The Evin Prison Bakers' Club

The Evin Prison Bakers' Club

Surviving Iran's
Most Notorious Prisons
in 16 Recipes

SEPIDEH GHOLIAN

TRANSLATED FROM THE PERSIAN
BY HESSAM ASHRAFI

Oneworld Publications Ltd does not provide any warranty, express or implied, regarding the content of recipes in this book. It is the reader's responsibility to determine the quality of any recipe or instructions provided for food preparation and to determine the nutritional value, if any, and safety of the preparation instructions.

The recipes presented are intended for entertainment and informational purposes and for use by persons having appropriate technical skill, at their own discretion and risk.

A ONEWORLD BOOK

First published in English by Oneworld Publications Ltd in 2025

First published in Persian by *IranWire* (London) under
the title *Ehzar Daval-paye Rosvaei Ba Paye-Sib*

Copyright © Sepideh Gholian, 2025
Translation copyright © Hessam Ashrafi

The moral right of Sepideh Gholian to be identified as the Author of this work has been asserted by her in accordance with the Copyright, Designs and Patents Act 1988

All rights reserved
Copyright under Berne Convention
A CIP record for this title is available from the British Library

ISBN 978-1-83643-030-8
eISBN 978-1-83643-029-2

Text designed and typeset by Tetragon, London
Printed and bound in Great Britain by Clays Ltd, Elcograf S.p.A.

No part of this publication may be reproduced, stored in a retrieval system, or transmitted, in any form or by any means, electronic, mechanical, photocopying, recording or otherwise, without the prior permission of the publishers.

The authorised representative in the EEA is eucomply OÜ,
Pärnu mnt 139b–14, 11317 Tallinn, Estonia
(email: hello@eucompliancepartner.com / phone: +33757690241)

Oneworld Publications Ltd
10 Bloomsbury Street
London WC1B 3SR
England

Stay up to date with the latest books,
special offers, and exclusive content from
Oneworld with our newsletter

Sign up on our website
oneworld-publications.com

CONTENTS

Introduction by Maziar Bahari ix

1. Curtain Up 3
2. The Disgrace 17
3. To Catch a Fish 39
4. The Diamond Stonecutter 53
5. The Year before the Nausea 63
6. And Now for the Shadow-Puppet Show 75
7. Paulina Salas 111
8. Saving Tuesdays 121
9. Sharing Dreams with Fatu 133
10. The National Library of Nostalgia 147
11. In Praise of Marzieh Amiri 159
12. Patisserie Pang 169

Appendix: A Tribute to Houman Jokar 177

For Zar Amir Ebrahimi,

a lesson in resistance against
the *Daval-pa* of disgrace

INTRODUCTION

By Maziar Bahari

I don't like clichés and I'm no fan of hyperbole. I tune out phrases like 'Literature will set you free', or that 'So-and-so is a true original', and make up my own mind. And yet here I am telling you that this book exemplifies how literature can liberate you, even while you're behind bars in Iran. And its author, the political prisoner Sepideh Gholian, is, without a trace of a lie, a true original.

In three decades of working as a journalist and documentary filmmaker, I've come to the conclusion that Iranian women are the country's best hope for social change. They awed the world with their bravery when they tore off their hijabs in the Woman, Life, Freedom protests in 2022. But for many decades before that, in fact since the Islamic Republic was first established in 1979, women have been on the frontlines of resistance, whether through private acts of rebellion or public protest, often at great personal cost.

Sepideh Gholian is the outstanding torchbearer of this tradition of resistance in the younger generation. Born in Dezful, Khuzestan, in 1994, as a 24-year-old student, she took a leading role in organising support for the Haft-Tappeh Sugarcane Complex strike in 2018. Since it was privatised in 2015, workers had to fight constant battles against job losses, unpaid wages and poor working conditions. Although strikes are illegal in Iran, Haft-Tappeh's trade union leaders managed to organise effective industrial action – even after being repeatedly targeted for persecution. Sepideh was not a worker, but she took on the role of reporting on the strike, organising meetings and building solidarity for the strikers in the local community and beyond.

Like millions of Iranians, I became fascinated by the young woman who swiftly became one of the public faces of the strike. We'd never seen an activist like Sepideh, whose bright blue hair could be glimpsed

INTRODUCTION

under her hijab, and whose very smile struck a blow against the Islamic Republic. That defiant and contagious smile, uncowed by any threat the regime could throw at her, seemed to make four decades of the Islamic Republic's relentless promotion of submission and solemnity crumble at once.

Amid the fourteen-day strike in 2018, Sepideh and other strike leaders were arrested at a peaceful protest. Months of torment ensued: detained without trial, Sepideh was brutally tortured in prison. In January 2019, the state broadcaster aired her 'confession', in which she 'admitted' to being a 'communist and Marxist' who somehow manipulated the striking workers into working with left-wing groups. The regime intended to shut her up. But on her release, she defied it once again.

Seated in front of an art installation she had made herself, Sepideh told the world about the insults, humiliation and beatings she endured. She spoke frankly about the sexual harassment she faced, and the way that interrogators weaponised sexual innuendoes to pile the pressure on prisoners – to make them feel disgraced and ashamed. She was not content simply to list these violations in the abstract – another account of a repressive regime refusing to respect basic human rights. She talked about her own experiences, her own traumas: she told her story to millions of Iranians inside Iran and in the diaspora. Many could see themselves in this brilliant young woman. And even more admired her uncompromising courage.

Sepideh has been arrested and released several times since 2018. The last time she was released in 2023, she shouted, 'Khamenei, you tyrant, we're going to put you in a grave,' denouncing Iran's 'Supreme' Leader Ayatollah Ali Khamenei, the highest spiritual and political authority in the country. She was arrested and jailed within a day. She is still in prison at the time of writing in August 2024.

I got to know Sepideh when she was temporarily released in 2019. I wanted to interview her for our website, IranWire.com. She gave the interview; but she also had other ideas. She wanted us to publish her first prison diary, *Tilapia Sucks the Blood of Hur al-Azim*; the title refers to how imports such as tilapia fish are draining the resources of Khuzestan province is southwest Iran. The book is a series of vignettes describing the lives

INTRODUCTION

of women in Iranian prisons. As a fellow prison diary author, detailing 107 days in solitary confinement in Iran in 2009, I couldn't help but be drawn to Sepideh's writing. She did not simply want to talk about herself; she wanted to tell the world about other prisoners' experiences, from Arab women persecuted for being Sunni to women facing unimaginable torture for crimes of survival. For many of these women, the only record of their lives is in Sepideh's book.

Here the activist Sepideh tries to understand the elaborate and labyrinthine system designed to oppress Iranian women and men. The women in *Tilapia* are not victims. Despite their harsh lives and the abuses they've suffered at the hands of their families and the authorities, they remain outspoken and playful.

Her first book was an activist's prison diary – an extended journalistic piece. But in this book, you meet Sepideh the writer. Even though Sepideh is barely thirty, it's no overstatement to hail this as a mature, literary work. I witnessed its birth and growth from a series of inchoate ideas into a unique masterpiece that only someone with Sepideh's creativity and resilience could write.

It all started with a text message: 'Maziar, I have an idea for a book: prison memoir and baking recipes.' I immediately wanted to know more. I report on human rights abuses every day – IranWire consistently raises awareness about conditions in Iranian prisons, and has done for years. But it burns you out; you become desensitised to the real suffering in these stories; you stop seeing the people's faces. Cooking is a new way in: it's an expression of people's personalities in the bitterest of circumstances. Suddenly each woman is no longer simply a victim of torture and oppression, but a rapper, a mother, a dancer.

For security reasons, I cannot tell you exactly how I received the different chapters of this book from Sepideh. All you need to know is that it took several people and multiple phone calls with different individuals, including Sepideh, to receive separate chapters by text or photos showing scraps of paper. We then had to type them up and figure out which piece belonged to which part of the book. The process would have been much simpler if the book was in a traditional format. But Sepideh, being Sepideh, made the process more challenging (and interesting) by insisting on placing

INTRODUCTION

the stories, footnotes and recipes alongside each other. We published the original Persian version of the book on IranWire.com, and in paperback in March 2024. Some of Sepideh's fellow prisoners report that even the guards enjoyed reading the book and were gripped by Sepideh's masterful writing.

If anyone wonders why we need literature, they need to read *The Evin Prison Bakers' Club*. Sepideh's voice breaks free from the cell, in which she still sits, and she can now introduce readers the world over to prisons full of the bravest women you will ever meet. And to their oppressors. Prisons are designed to be impenetrable, to isolate someone from the world – but Sepideh tears down the walls and lets us in.

My involvement in drafting the final book was limited to helping Sepideh clarify some of her ideas and to making her vision of the different elements – such as footnotes, recipes and drawings – work as a whole. Publishing the book would have been impossible without the help of numerous people, especially Samaneh and Mehdi, Sepideh's older sister and brother. Like many Iranian activists, Sepideh would not be who she is without the support of her family. Since the world came to know Sepideh, we have also become acquainted with her family, who fight alongside her and tell the world about what she has endured. Rose Jafry did an amazing job editing the Persian text. Hessam Ashrafi brilliantly translated it into English and made sure the English version reflects Sepideh's ideas and expressions. Hannah Somerville and Mitchell Albert were superb editors of Hessam's translation.

I must also thank my colleagues at IranWire.com. Without their dedication to reporting news of Iran fairly but diligently, we would not be able to help writers and activists such as Sepideh find a home for their articles, videos, cartoons and books.

Finally, thank you Sepideh-jan, for trusting me with the book. Working with you has been one of the most joyous moments of my professional life. Your dedication to fighting for the rights of the Iranian people has inspired me and millions of Iranians to follow your example however we can. I am honoured to introduce your beautiful, heartbreaking stories and recipes to English-speaking audiences.

Woman, Life, Freedom!

MAZIAR BAHARI is a journalist and documentary filmmaker. He is the founder of IranWire.com, where the original Persian version of *The Evin Prison Bakers' Club* was published.

The Evin Prison Bakers' Club

ONE

Curtain Up

I am not a good baker. All right, I'm not a baker at all. Like a lot of things, I do it without being skilled at it. Like writing. I've never been a writer, and I doubt I'll ever be one.

The baking started a little while before my first arrest. Back then I was already a detainee in my own home. Baking allowed me to forget about the beatings I received for being a woman. And, naturally, I was a very rebellious woman.

Everything took on a new meaning after I was arrested in November 2018. In the course of that single, harrowing night, I was shunted between five different detention centres. At one point, as they were moving me from one car to the next, blindfolded and surrounded by male security agents, I reached for the door handle, intending to throw myself out. Right at that moment, my dear friend Sepideh Kashani came to mind.* (I'll tell you more about Kashi and her husband Houman in Chapter Ten.) It occurred to me that, at the end of whatever road this was, I might see her, and that together we might bake something nice for her husband Houman. The thought made me euphoric. I retracted my hand.

You might well ask, *Isn't prison ... prison? How the hell could you be making confectionery there?* And you would be correct. But if baking badly is an inalienable part of who you are, then you can do it anytime, anywhere, and – yes – in any kind of prison.

Even without gas. Boiling water goes into a flask; butter is put into a plastic bag; digestive biscuits are ground down to a powder with the back of a sieve. Mash them together, then attend to the jelly and other such things. (Much easier if there *is* gas, mind you.) So it was that on the women's ward of Evin Prison, side by

---

* Sepideh Kashani is a conservationist and activist. Together with her husband Houman Jokar and other environmentalists, including Niloufar Bayani, Sam Rajabi and Kavous Seyed-Emami, she was arrested by the Islamic Revolutionary Guard Corps' Intelligence Organisation in January 2018. All of them were subsequently jailed for 'espionage'.

side with my dear Niloufar Bayani,* after a barrage of repeated requests, entreaties and follow-ups, we got our hands on our weapons of choice: culinary utensils and, crucially, a tin for tarts and pies. They were plainly not going to release us so we were going to get a tart tin out of them, at least.

Later on, in Bushehr Prison, I also sought refuge in baking. The environment there was different. You couldn't so much as whisper into the ears of your fellow inmates without reprisal. But I made use of my 'privilege' as a political prisoner to set up a kitchen. In the midst of all that suffering, I actually had a few decent days. Of course, they never lasted, and I am still haunted by nightmares from that time.

Let's move on.

Ultimately, I came to realise that, baking aside, there are a lot of things you can't do in an endemically repressive patriarchal system. I saw that I wasn't much more than a toy. I'd been beaten, humiliated and shamed. My heart explodes whenever I remember.

---

* Niloufar Bayani was held in solitary confinement for eight months after her arrest in January 2018. Following a trial held behind closed doors, she was jailed for ten years for 'espionage'.

My sister Mahin died.* During my furlough, I was at the edge of an abyss. Everything would have been over for me, had it not been for her love.

Let's move on.

Those bygone days and bygone lives play out now before me like a horror movie. Never could I have dreamed they would execute Somayeh, one day after we'd cried together and eaten a cake at the foot of our bed in prison.† And never could I have dreamed that after handing a cream puff to Maryam Akbari Monfared, just *one day* after we'd done the New Year's house cleaning together in eager anticipation of the Nowruz festivities, they'd transfer her to another prison.

Back then I used to call Maryam my 'mother'. When I heard other young female inmates calling her 'Mum'

---

* Thirty-year-old Mahin Boland Karami was a full-time worker in Bushehr Prison, as punishment for working as a *kolbar*. *Kolbars* are couriers who carry goods on their backs over the Iran–Iraq border to scrape a living. The mountain route is perilous, and dozens of them are shot on sight by Iranian border guards every year. This type of work is prevalent in Iranian Kurdistan due to the high levels of unemployment. Mahin died of Covid-19.
† Thirty-three-year-old Somayeh Shahbazi Jahrouii was convicted of murdering a man who her relatives said had tried to rape her. She was hanged in Sepidar Women's Prison in Ahvaz on 4 December 2019.

too, I'd feel my heart, a block of ice, thawing. I could never be jealous – far from it. It was Maryam's miracle that she was a mother to us all. But the day she was banished, I did feel my heart turn to ice again. 'I love you so much,' she whispered into my ear. The sorrow was fathoms deep.

As it happened, they transferred me too, the very next day. It was a mercy. I don't think I could have dealt with Maryam's absence if they'd kept me there. In another absurd twist of fate, I'm now back in Evin Prison, and I still can't even look at the spot where she and I once had our bed.

Let's move on.

In Bushehr, the person I lost was Mahin. You miss each person in a different way; each loss brings a new kind of hurt, both physically and psychologically. When I touched my sister's foot in those last moments, it was so, so cold. And right now, as I remember her and as I write this, my own hands are going ice cold.

Let's move on.

Recipe 1

Tres leches ('three milks') cake for Mahin Boland Karami

◆ ◆ ◆

Mahin Boland Karami works full-time in prison. The mop is broken and she has to spend hours bent double cleaning the toilets, the corridors, and everywhere else with a broken implement. When the working day is done, she twists her hips and shows off her Kurdish dancing. No wonder her blood sugar levels have dropped.

'I want a very, very sweet cake. I don't have enough money for a cream puff. Give me something else this time.'

'OK. It'll be ready in about two hours.'

This was probably the last conversation Mahin and another prisoner had about pastries. Not long afterwards, the kitchen was shut down, and Mahin froze to death.

This is a treat of Spanish origin, and easy to prepare.* If you invite someone to enjoy it with you, don't forget to tell them that, at the first hearing of her trial, Mahin defended herself in Kurdish. Then emphasise that she was a real 'Leyla Zana' – a Kurdish member of the Turkish parliament who was jailed for fifteen years for doing the same thing. And don't forget

---

* The origins of *tres leches* cake lie in Latin America, although there is debate about whether its genesis was in Mexico, where soaked desserts were popular in the mid-nineteenth century, or Nicaragua. When Nestlé opened up factories in Mexico in the 1930s, it printed a recipe for *tres leches* on the back of its cans of condensed and evaporated milk.

to follow this up with this poem by the Iraqi-Kurdish poet Sherko Bekas:

> In the land of the gallows and ashes and spoils
> you are the sister of the motherland's evergreens,
> and when you were being devoured by the whales and monsters,
> from the sun of today's women,
> from the infernal orators of today,
> there were none who had not tied their tongues out of fear,
> there were none who had not hidden their voices under the pillow
> and their courage in the closet.
> Today is the shining day of your glowing hair.
> Today is the eighth of March.
> Each year on this day,
> that beautiful dove from Kirkuk
> takes to the sky
> and lands on the windowsill of Leyla Zana's prison.

This cake is indeed very sweet. But don't let that worry you; it is delicious. Arabs are probably responsible for the high sugar content of Spanish cakes.

CAKE INGREDIENTS

190g flour190g sugar
1 tsp baking powder5 eggs
115g butter½ tsp vanilla essence

MILK MIXTURE INGREDIENTS

200ml milk200ml clotted cream
200ml condensed milk

DIRECTIONS

Mix the butter and sugar until light and creamy. Add the eggs one by one, followed by the vanilla essence, flour and baking powder. Pour the mixture into greased tins. Place in a preheated oven for 30–40 minutes at 180°C. When completely cool, use a toothpick to poke little holes all over the top of the cake. Whip the double cream and mix thoroughly with the milk and condensed milk. Pour the whole lot over the top of the cake. Leave in the refrigerator for a day or so for the milk mixture to penetrate. Decorate your cake with whipped cream, fruit, or cinnamon.

CURTAIN UP

I WAS OUT OF PRISON when I got the news that Makieh had died.* At first I didn't believe it. I asked after her everywhere I could think of. There was no information available. Either people didn't have it, or they just wouldn't give it to me.

At the height of this fact-finding mission, I went to the gates of Sepidar Women's Prison in Ahvaz. I'd seen a movie in prison called *At the End of 8th Street*. In one scene, the actress Taraneh Alidoosti stands outside a prison cradling a pair of trainers belonging to her brother, who's just been sentenced to death. I felt as though I was re-enacting that scene, squatting there, hugging my knees and asking everybody who passed by about Makieh.

Finally, her cellmate's family gave me definitive news. Makieh was dead. She hadn't just died, either: she'd been killed. As I stood there, in front of the gates of Sepidar Prison, I felt that my back was bent abruptly.

---

* Makieh Neisi, an ethnic Arab mother of three in her thirties, was arrested in November 2019 during anti-government protests in Iran. She was accused of collaborating with ISIS, and subjected to sexual torture. She died on 14 December 2020, in the quarantine ward of Sepidar Women's Prison, after being denied adequate medical care.

It was Makieh's body weighing me down. I felt as if I'd never stand upright again.

It's strange to lose so many, in just three years. It feels as though one hundred years passed just between Makieh and Mahin.

But let's move on.

I suffer from a guilty conscience. I'm not sure how I'm supposed to bear it. You see, I tell myself I was complicit in the deaths of two people. If I hadn't mouthed off about how Arabs are abused the moment I left Sepidar Prison, I might not have been rearrested, and then I'd certainly have been by Makieh's side. I'd never have allowed her to be left alone on the quarantine ward. My exile from Ahvaz was costly in the extreme.

I tell myself that if I'd held my tongue in the face of harassment by the then-president of the Prisons Organisation, Haj Mohammadi, that video wouldn't have been posted of me shouting online, and the prison fight in which Mahin had to defend me might not have happened; then they wouldn't have retaliated by taking her life while she was laid up with Covid-19.

My hands freeze again.

CURTAIN UP

Let's move on.

I never abandoned baking, all the way down this tortuous road. It's hard to be a woman, hard enough even for me, and I don't know if I can continue to bear it. Worse, Makieh was an Arab and Mahin Kurdish, and that makes it harder still.

If you're not a baker or a pastry chef, these recipes might be of use to you. Try them all, if you can. And while you're making them, remember the women from Kurdistan, Khuzestan, and all over Iran, who created them. Remember them always, and you'll understand, as I do, that baking isn't just about preparing sweets and eating them. There are other things; I still don't know all of them, though.

I make baked goods with my dear friend Niloufar Bayani. If you encounter any problem with our recipes in this book, and if I'm not in prison at the time, please notify me on Instagram or X. If I am in prison, send a letter to whatever facility they're holding me in. I had to write all these recipes in haste, in the two months before I was taken back to Evin Prison. Blame my rudimentary prose on this, not on any lack of talent. (Joking!)

One day, when our people are victorious, I'll bake you a cake in the streets of Ahvaz. That day isn't far off now.

I hope we can bring it about together.

TWO
The Disgrace

She is pregnant. She doesn't know it yet. What will happen when she does?

A pack of card-carrying murderers handcuff her and take her to the car. They don't know that she's pregnant yet, either. Wait and see what happens when they learn that she is. Even the prospect of it, from all the way over here in the third person, is terrifying, never mind the reality.

Inside the prison cell, the young woman dives into a corner. Nausea has made her desperate. There's no window, no water to drink, no place to throw up. There's nothing but silence and death, and herself. She is freezing cold, wrapped in foul-smelling blankets overrun with bedbugs. Days like this are going to repeat themselves over and over, with a few minor variations. Little by little, she'll get used to the reek of the blankets.

Desperately tired, sometimes she'll fall unconscious; the sounds of the agents' footsteps will awaken her, and it'll go on. Everything is going to repeat itself, and she already knows it all perfectly, from the smell of the blankets to the itching and the gashes left by the bedbugs' stings. She knows that she is going to piss herself.

These things she knows, but not that she is pregnant. Not at the moment, anyhow. Right now she's preoccupied solely by these repetitive events, so repetitive and predictable she can even tell which bedbug was the last to sting her in the groin. Hell, she knows the total number of bedbugs in the cell. Not only this: she knows the woman in the neighbouring cell is refusing to confess, and that's why the door to her cell will never open. This neighbour suspects what she doesn't yet realise; that she is pregnant. That ignorance won't last. The young woman pulls up her blanket. She will get used to the smell of vomit.

They take her to another car, still unaware that she is pregnant. They beat her and throw a thick piece of sacking over her head. She and the faces that she cannot see have nothing in common – except for the fact that not one of them knows she is pregnant.

THE DISGRACE

With a bag on her head and a body turning frail, the young woman is driven off towards an unknown destination. The hours crawl by. In the car, she can't discern whether or not they're heading for hotter or colder climes, into sun or into shadow. It hardly seems to matter. There are five individuals in the car. One of them is hidden in the belly of the young woman, who is our story.

Now she wakes with a start. She implores God for the two-thousandth time not to let her be disgraced today. Maybe all women wake up thinking this. Disgrace is always right around the corner. It's dormant in their throats, in their minds. Will she be disgraced today? It's a roll of the dice.

The young woman is gaunt. Not so very long ago, one of her sisters died. Not long after that, a second sister followed the first into the grave. News of the second sister's death had yet to be confirmed to her when a third sister passed away.

All her sisters were young and tall, and all had sonorous voices. The first was Somayeh, who had a round face and jet-black hair. The second was Makieh, who had eyes the colour of honey and a scorched chest:

her brother-in-law had burned it with boiling water. Makieh's life had been bereft of colour, save for her eyes. With those honey-coloured eyes, she'd witnessed her brother's murder. Her chest never stopped burning. Perhaps it hadn't stopped burning, even at the end. Her infant child's name was 'Halva'.*

The third sister, Mahin, happened to love *halva* as well. It had been her constant sweet companion during pregnancy. Mahin had been in the habit of twisting the *halva* around her finger and licking it off. Finger-twist *halva* is a real thing that comes from Bushehr. It contains equal parts flour and sugar, and also a lot of oil. If you're diabetic, run for the hills. But if you're pregnant like Mahin and have a craving for sweets, it's a dream come true.

---

* *Halva*, a popular confectionery of Persian origin, consists of a thick paste made from fried wheat flour, butter and oil, flavoured with saffron, rosewater and sugar.

Recipe 2

Finger-twist halva

◆ ◆ ◆

Finger-twist *halva* comes from the Persian Gulf city of Bushehr, and is so called because you can stretch it, wrap it around your finger, then pop it straight into your adorable mouth. It's comforting, soft and smooth. Play a folk song from that region. All the ingredients are combined in equal amounts, so it's easy to remember.

INGREDIENTS

1 cup water
1 cup rosewater
1 cup sugar
1 cup cooking oil
1 cup flour

1 cup saffron ... No, stop, just kidding, we're not trying to bankrupt you. Just a bit of ground saffron will be fine.

DIRECTIONS

Mix the sugar, water, rosewater and saffron together, and heat on the stove until the sugar is completely dissolved. That's your syrup. Now, in a separate pan, toast the flour and slowly add the oil, then cook this paste until it turns a gorgeous brown. Then add the syrup, little by little. Mix thoroughly and flip it about until all the oil is emulsified. It is delicious.

◆ ◆ ◆

Mahin, 'Barefaced Mahin' as she called herself, was the young woman's third sister, and she died in her arms. Today the young woman still breaks down when she remembers how it happened. Mahin was thirty years old, and she worked as a *kolbar*. She'd ended up carrying a load belonging to a man who had made her his slave. In order to pay her son's school expenses, and in return for a pittance, she'd agreed to carry a mountain of crystal meth around her belly. A pregnancy of another kind. Ultimately, she was caught and sent to prison. The man whose cargo she had carried was not.

On the day she died, Mahin couldn't breathe. She needed oxygen. She didn't get it. Exactly 20 seconds before it happened, the young woman kissed her shoulder and asked her forgiveness. Mahin had previously saved the young woman's life, and for that infraction she was now being denied medical care. She should never have saved her. Because of what she'd done, for that unforgivable sin, Mahin the Kurd followed the first two sisters into the Valley of Death.

In the end all three of the woman's sisters were killed by suffocation in some form. Somayeh was hanged.

Then Mahin and Makieh were starved of oxygen, one after the other. Now the woman is all alone, and she fears that she, too, will die of suffocation. It happens to a lot of women. What about you? Have you ever lost a sister, because she couldn't breathe?

The woman cannot cry. Three sisters lost, in two years. And yet she keeps thinking about baking, just like the sisters who were suffocated always used to think about baking. In the corridors of the courthouse, the day before Somayeh was strangled at the gallows, she'd cried in her mother's arms. 'Mum,' she had wailed. 'I can't breathe!' And her mother had replied: 'Nor me.' It seems the condition is hereditary. If not now, it will come for us all in the end.

In the car, they pull the bag off the woman's head, and she realises that she won't be going home again. 'Help!' she screams. 'They're taking my home away from me!' The agents pummel her in response. Other, earlier affronts come to mind. She remembers the other alleyways, the other towns, even the other detention centres, all of which were at least filled with the voices of her own people. *Will I ever go back?* the woman asks herself, and thinks vainly of poplar trees.

The floor in her cell is freezing, and there's no ventilation. In all likelihood, she will be here for a long time to come. She wants to claw at the walls. True, she's been in this cell before, but she didn't feel nausea back then. She's vomited twice in the past two hours. *It must be a side effect of the hunger strike*, she tells herself.

At sunset that same day, in the southern warmth and seasonal breeze, she's taken from solitary confinement out into the prison's recreation yard, in absolute silence. The yard is clean; there's nobody there. *Dey Hengo must have cleaned up*, she thinks.* She doesn't hear a sound. Where are the inmates? There's nobody here.

This absolute silence conveys a message to the young woman. Everybody is to be treated as her enemy now, irrespective of what they believe. If they're not hostile, they'll meet the same end as Mahin. *Mahin, Mahin, Mahin*. The woman turns Mahin's name over in her mind, then throws up.

She tells herself it must be because of the grief. Why, then, has she not been able to shed a tear for Mahin

---

* The author describes Dey Hengo ('Mother Hengameh') in Chapter Three.

all this time? She doesn't have an answer. Instead, she recalls the last time they danced. It was around the same time of day as now, and as warm and windy as it is this evening. They'd managed to dance together for a full hour. *We all danced for each other,* the young woman thinks.

In the end, she makes her way around the yard ten times. Is she going to survive this? Doubtful. She thinks about the days ahead, about her nausea. She gazes at the corner of the yard. Mahin's body lay there for days, waiting for the ambulance. Not so long before that, she'd been dancing just a few short paces away. *They'd managed to dance together for an hour.* This is very important to the young woman just now.

The window for 'recreation' closes, and she is returned to her cell. Then the agents come for her and tell her it's time to go. This time she doesn't ask any questions. Her body isn't up to it.

It's so cold now, as though a heavy snow has fallen. She gazes at the lights on the dashboard. She smiles, but she has to close her eyes. There it is again: she feels sick. They take more pictures of her face. This time she doesn't ask why. It's very cold.

Our pregnant young woman has been down this road before, and not just metaphorically. Down this exact same corridor. It's almost funny. Over the past five nights she must have been searched fifty times, but not one person has figured out that there's something hidden in her belly. It would be a shadow as dark as death if they did, a final testament to disgrace.

The young woman has experienced disgrace plenty of times before. But how to deal with this? Disgrace is a *Daval-pa*: if you don't fight it once it catches you, it'll destroy you entirely.*

What happens when they find out that she is pregnant? They'll probably inform her family. The very first thing her father will do is cut her mother's throat in her sleep. A long time ago, he threatened to do this over a different scandal their daughter had caused. Then her brother will do the same to her sister. Then, at least, the young woman – with a baby in her belly – can take a five-day leave of absence to observe the funeral rites.

---

* The *Daval-pa* is a parasitic monster in Persian mythology, with leather strap-like appendages for legs, which are used as tentacles to grasp hold of and enslave human beings.

THE DISGRACE

She'll have no choice but to give birth. With enough effort made, she might get to visit her father and brother in prison. Of course, they'll refuse to see her. The brother will have pardoned the father, and the father will have pardoned the brother.* Ultimately, they'll get five years each, the same sentence the disgraced young woman is serving. All the while, in mourning for her mother and sister, she'll have to stare down at the bastard child who caused their collective ruin.

After the inspection, the young woman is returned to her cell and throws up again. If they'd taken their time over it, she'd have had no choice but to throw up where she stood. The moon climbs high into the sky. The world is cold and dark. Mahin is underground, as are Somayeh and Makieh. There are others who'd prefer to be underground even while still above it. And there is this young woman, in the corner of her prison cell, who'd managed to get pregnant the first time she'd made love. But she doesn't know it yet.

---

* Under Iran's Islamic Penal Code, the next of kin of a murder victim is entitled to *qisas* (retribution), or retaliation in kind. But they can also order that the murder charge be dropped. The perpetrators of so-called honour killings are often absolved in this way by sympathetic relatives, who have sometimes also been complicit in the crime.

She had never really known what intercourse was. She had never really known what *pregnancy* was. Nobody had taught her anything. As a consequence, she suspects anything and everything else: ulcers, coronavirus, nerves, food poisoning from the liver she ate a full month earlier, the hunger strike, Mahin, Makieh …

They bring a new woman into the adjacent cell. Her name is Maryam. She cries non-stop all day, and the young woman throws up continuously all day, in concert. Maryam's story is just as repetitive, from the bedbugs to the detention centre to the full-body searches. She's been charged with drug dealing. She was arrested instead of her husband, and it's unclear from her story who actually had the drugs in their possession. Either way, there's nobody to take care of her small children. She's been told they will be placed in the care of the Welfare Organisation. Maryam is at her wits' end. She doesn't know where her husband is.

The young woman can guess just by looking into Maryam's eyes how long she will be confined, here or in other squalid cells. She knows they'll hold Maryam for so long her hair will turn the same colour as her teeth. She knows that soon they'll confiscate everything that belongs to Maryam. She knows Maryam's husband will never return. She even knows that the government officials don't want him to. They aren't troubled by the act of drug dealing per se, but by the fact that someone other than themselves was making an income from it. Narcotics are within their purview, and they don't want competition; what they want is a scapegoat, and that's Maryam.

Eventually, Maryam was convinced to cooperate with them under the impression that if she confessed, she'd be released and able to see her children again. The young woman knows it never happens like that, but she doesn't say as much to Maryam. Naturally, she lies, like they all do. 'Don't cry! One of these days they'll set you free,' she exhorts, then throws up extravagantly, losing the last remnants of the food she had eaten two days earlier. Then she trundles back to her ward, to her own enclosure.

From under her blindfold and flowery *chador*, she recognises each of the decorated floor tiles, and as such can make her way along without tripping up. The climate's always the same in here. Neither warm nor cold.

The young woman is alarmed she's losing so much hair. It carpets the floor. She sleeps on it where it lies, and sometimes braids the bits that have fallen out.

They've come for her. The young woman gets dressed and puts her *chador* back on. Blindfolded again, she makes her way past the agents and back onto the familiar painted floor tiles. Going along the corridors, she thinks she can hear the sound of rain. But the air itself hasn't changed, and it's still silent.

Up ahead she can see the legs of an orderly row of chairs. Four iron chair legs, two human feet in plastic slippers, peeking out from the ends of two grey trouser legs. They're always there, making her wonder whether or not they're part of the decoration of the corridor together with the floor tiles. Perhaps they sit there for hours, days, even years on end. Perhaps they freeze and defrost. There's something about the sight of the four chair legs, the two human feet and the plastic slippers, that all-pervading silence, that makes her feel sick again. Right there and then in the middle of the hallway, she could do it. But a female guard shouts out a warning: 'The sound of vomiting is forbidden!'

Finally, in the next room, she sits down heavily on the wooden chair. They want her to write something, but she throws up all over the papers. They're furious. The young woman's only weapon now is this technicolour yawn. She wants to void her stomach over all the names they're demanding she write. Because she doesn't know that she is pregnant, she tells the agents she's got a tummy bug. Then she drags herself back down the silent hallway to her cell. She counts the grey legs as she passes. All present and correct.

On rejoining Maryam, she tells her about her craving for sweets. Maryam bursts into tears and says her children love sweets, too. Maryam says she's not had her period in two months and is terrified; she wonders aloud, dismayed even as the words form in her mouth, whether or not she might not be pregnant. Then she starts talking about her husband and her children, about her first pregnancy and how she missed her period then, too (who'd have thought it), and finally calls out to the female guard: 'Please, can you get me a pregnancy test from the clinic?'

The guard refuses the request. She explains that, first, Maryam must make the request; then she's got to 'follow up' on it. The young woman can't bear the words *follow up*, and throws up on the floor. Maryam pivots on the spot. 'Perhaps it's *you* that's pregnant!'

The fear that engulfs the young woman then is new, unfamiliar. She denies it, and instead asks Maryam: 'What's pregnancy like?' Maryam explains that a pregnant woman has a nervous breakdown.

This would be the end of everything. This scandal, the wooden chair facing the wall, those grey legs, this cell. They'll probably do to her what they did to Leila Rotbeh: gather all the grey legs together in a room to watch her giving birth. Like when Sakineh was giving birth to her child.* All the nurses burst into laughter. They shook the hospital foundations with their shouts: '*The bastard is born!*'

The young woman is transferred to another detention centre, with slightly different ceramic tiles. She is blindfolded, can't see the new investigators, can only hear their voices. They want her to describe her personal

---

* This refers to Sakineh Sagoori, who was thirty-four years old and gave birth in prison. In Sepideh Gholian's prison diaries, available on IranWire, Sakineh was made to 'confess' that her newborn child was an ISIS member.

relationships. She wonders if they've installed a camera in her belly, if they know she's pregnant. Perhaps it's the details of it they're after, though she's not even sure what's happened herself.

The town, her relatives, the town, her relatives go round and round in her head. She has to be certain about any pregnancy before they are. She has to get back to her cell and ask Maryam for help. But they've brought her here now. What if they don't take her back? They've said they will.

The invisible interrogator starts asking questions again. The more personal the answers she gives, the happier he sounds. The young woman cradles the unproven child and wonders what she can do to force them to take her back. In a moment of inspiration, she picks up the chair and pounds it against the wall. She pounds herself against the wall too, for good measure, and bangs the wall with her hands. Rips off her mask. The interrogator doesn't know what to do. He fumbles for his mask, to remain invisible, and shouts to her: 'Pull the blindfold back over your eyes, woman!'

The woman throws her own belly down onto the ground, seven times. She wants to escape this scandal.

They chain up her legs. She screams that she wants her own cell. The more she screams, the more chains they bring for her. A guard returns her to the cell. The woman ignores all the threats: it's worked. Now she has to get back to Maryam.

When she does, Maryam is shocked by her condition. 'Did you do the test?' the young woman asks. It's still in the 'follow-up' process, Maryam replies. While they wait, they scheme.

The young woman suggests that she gives Maryam her own urine for testing, so she can check the result and then accidentally 'drop' the test kit, tell the guards – and, that way, get hold of a second one for herself. She empties out a small bottle of shampoo in the bathroom, replaces the contents with her own urine, and gives it to Maryam.

It's a good plan. Several 'follow-ups' later, both Maryam and the bottle are taken away for testing. It's the weekend, so no blood tests are available, just this more rudimentary method. Maryam steals into the bathroom with the test kit. A few minutes later, the young woman's disgrace is there on the strip.

Maryam is scared. This could mean several people will be killed. But, as promised, the test kit falls from her hand into the toilet and she tells the agent, who explodes in rage. After the shouting subsides, she gets her second test. This one is negative.

Maryam returns to her cell. At first she wants to lie to the young woman, but she also knows that she'd want the truth were she single and in this position. And the young woman isn't going to see the open skies for a long time. So, she tells her kindly that she is 'disgraced'. The young woman turns pale, wails, and falls to the floor. Then she begs Maryam to keep her secret.

They call the young woman back to the interrogation room. Now she knows her belly's got a foetus in it, it feels like a sea encircling one solitary little fish. But she, too, is the fish; the sea is her country. She wants to give the sea back to the parched lands and dried-up marshes of her native town, and the fish to the Karun River for the fisherman Ali to catch. She sees the picture of her pregnancy on the ceramic tiles. She tries to ignore the disgrace. She'd be glad to throw both foetus and the act that made it into the sea.

Over the floor tiles, past the chair legs, back to the blank papers. Now, though, she doesn't say anything. What she's thinking is: *You still don't know, and you will never know, that I am pregnant.* Now the young woman wants to control the game. The interrogator warns she'll be sent to solitary if she continues her silence. That suits her very well. She mustn't ever see Maryam again.

It's better in solitary confinement. She's less likely to be exposed, although there's still the possibility that Maryam will stay loyal to the tears that they have shed together. The woman thinks about what might come next, and how to stop it. If the child is born, it will be the end of them all.

THREE
To Catch a Fish

THE WOMAN REVIEWS her plan. First, she's resolved to throw up quietly and secretly from now on. Now that her pregnancy is proven, she needs to hide its symptoms until the day the fish dies. Between throwing up and the death of the fish, she is going to write three letters: to her lover, to her unborn child and to her dear Somayeh. She reviews and records the letters in her mind.

FIRST LETTER

Hello!

Carrying a foetus over ceramic tiles is hard, very hard in a solitary cell and much harder in an interrogation room. But do you know what's going to be harder than any of that? Abortion in the solitary cell. I've carried this child, the fruit of my love, my youth, and my womanhood, down the corridors of Ward 241, down Ward 209, through the Criminal Investigations Department, down the roads and in the cold, without ever knowing of its existence. It was a miracle I even learned about it. I'm frustrated no end by my lack of awareness and neglect of my own body. This child is a mass murderer before it's even been born. And now I, its mother, have to kill it.

I've been thinking about how to do it since this morning. If there's even a one percent chance that it might survive, death will have its claws around my throat, and my sister's. Even if I were married, I wouldn't have considered giving birth. To be a woman is frightful – and living, more so. The child's mother is already shackled and chained. But the child itself?

I had a chat with my child, my *halva* fish.* Saying '*halva*' reminds me of Makieh, even if I'm talking about *halva* fish. Everything's blended together in my brain. My *halva*, Makieh's *halva*, the kind of *halva*

---

* *Halva*, as noted, is a type of confectionery. But it's also the Persian word for *pomfret*, a species of butterfish beloved in Indo-Pacific and West Asian regions for its slightly sweet flavour.

TO CATCH A FISH

Mahin loves, and the fish called *halva*. I want to pull it out of my belly and fricassée it, Dey Hengo-style. My arms are pretty strong now. I could catch it, I'm sure.

Let me tell you about Dey Hengo. *Dey* means *mother* in the Bushehr dialect, and *Hengo* is the diminutive of the name 'Hengameh'. Dey Hengo, Mother Hengameh, is an inmate on the women's ward of Bushehr Prison. She's an indelible part of the place. I'm picturing her dishevelled appearance and her fine, grey hair right now – are you? She's been held for six years so far, because she owes 60 million *tomans* (just over $1000).

Life on the women's ward of Bushehr Prison goes something like this: first thing in the morning, after the inmate count and morning exercises (which you do in a *chador*), we make the beds, then leave the ward to take part in workshops, recite prayers and repent. You can't come back to the ward until noon. When you do, you have to quickly eat lunch and take a nap. We're not allowed to socialise. But Dey Hengo isn't allowed to eat with the others any more. She's really sick. Her left arm is paralysed. She lost her young daughter, and she's been breathing in this hell for six years.

Want to know why Dey Hengo had her first stroke? Because she lost her job as charwoman. No, really. Dey Hengo cleans the toilet, the exercise yard and, until recently, the prison guards' underwear. That was her only respite: washing the guards' underwear. Time and again, they tried to take it away from her. I remember the day it happened at last. She'd been talking to me in whispers, and she'd been seen. They called her over and told her: 'You are no longer going to do the laundry. Shirin will do it instead.' Dey Hengo fell to pieces. She had a stroke. The right side of her face was lopsided for a while. It was horrific.

Dey Hengo buried her child not so long ago. One of the guards here slapped her, at the age of fifty-three, because her breast had fissured due to extreme diabetes and she couldn't wear the underwear as prescribed. Her only consolation had been to wash theirs.

If you'd been born a woman, you might have experienced some of the things Dey Hengo has. I'm going to have to bury my child unclothed, just like Dey Hengo did her youngest daughter Afsaneh. We each carried a foetus in our belly.

TO CATCH A FISH

Dey Hengo loves cooking. She was desperate to make a *gheliyeh** with *halva* fish. Then they shut the kitchen down.

But let's move on. Dey Hengo's recipe for *gheliyeh* looks like this:

> I write the story of my youth and my old age.
>
> Greetings to my lovely daughter. I don't know which part of my life to write about. I got married in 1981 when I was thirteen. Then I had a child, my precious Afshin. My husband always liked my cooking, especially the *gheliyeh* and other fish dishes. This is what you do. First, fry the onion and then add a little garlic. Then add fresh herbs and a spoonful of tomato paste. Add tamarind juice, with just a little flour. Wash the fish in water and put it in the pot. Right after it starts to boil, lower the flame until the fricassée is done. When you're ready for lunch, eat it seasoned with ground pepper and a bunch of herbs (see the note, below). Mix some drinks to go with it, then take a pleasing nap.

---

* *Gheliyeh* is a spicy fish stew from southern Iran, flavoured with fresh coriander, parsley and dried fenugreek.

Yes, I had a life that was both difficult and good. Even with the hardships, my life was so good. It was good that I was by my children's side. When Afshin turned four, I had Iman, and when Iman was six months old, I fell pregnant with Afsaneh ... A few years after Afsaneh was born, I fell pregnant with Ahmad. All in all, I was very happy and my husband was with me. But in 2006, I lost all of this happiness. I was never happy, not even for a moment, ever again. Yes, I had a happy life that ended badly.

In the name of God

Greetings, my daughter. I hope you have a good night, and that I'll never see a teardrop on your face, because no mother can bear her child's tears. Yes, you are the daughter of Dey Hengo. Be strong and stand firm in all that you do. I am proud of you. God is in your heart, and you share your heart with everybody. I love you not in words alone, but from deep within my heart.

I've made the *gheliyeh*. It tastes wonderful. Pass it on it to your friends. But don't make it yourself! Wait for me.

I will catch the fish inside me. My hands have become as strong as a fisherman's. Once I've pulled out the *halva* fish, I'll fricassée it just like Dey Hengo. Our child will become a part of us again. Dey Hengo will flow within us as well. I've washed the bowl completely clean, and I promise you I'll turn *halva* into *gheliyeh* before they find out and kill us all. Dey Hengo is never going to be able to repay her debt, and one of these days they'll take her off cleaning duties altogether because she smiled at somebody, and she'll have another stroke and expire in silence like Mahin. This is the world of mothers, which you have never experienced and never will. I want to reproach you for this, but I can't. My love doesn't allow for it.

It's been raining here. Perhaps you've also seen the rain. I have sung this song very quietly a few times now. I walk around with no purpose, and laugh for no reason. I'm tired of running. Sit down with me, so my bones don't crumble. These past few years have been filled with fatigue. Too many nightmares, beatings and lost loved ones. The light of the sky has died inside me. My motherland has died, and I'm a woman in exile. Being so far from home has killed me. No piece of the land is mine, and I long for the sky. I was the fish and you were the sea. The pain of separation has driven me insane.

What happens now doesn't matter, really. Saying your name makes my hands safe. My body is protected when I remember your body. My heart soars in the sun when I remember your laughter. I would not be exaggerating if I said that everything I have, I have found in the depths of your eyes: love, my home, my womanhood. I could cross any number of empty corridors. I could strike out for any horizon, in my slippers, on the ceramics. I have imagined how much weaker my feet would be, had it not been for your kisses on them. Something moved inside me then. It was you, under my flowery *chador*. My dearest, I remember you so well. I remember every moment. I have tightly embraced the corpses of my sisters behind your eyelids, and kissed them with fire in my heart. My heart was on fire because I didn't get to kiss them at the last moment. Your eyelids were their corpses, and kissing them ended my agony.

Forever yours,

                        Your Nightmare-Addled Lover

TO CATCH A FISH

SECOND LETTER

My child, the fish, Halva, Fricassée,

   I cast you into my mouth and taste you. I cast you back into the belly from whence you came. Your body shall become my body, and you shall not be released into this world. Go to Somayeh, eat chocolate cake with her. Sit down and enjoy her dancing. You shall not be given to the world. I will taste you in my mouth, I will place your heart in mine. I will savour your eyes in my memories. I will sweeten you with lotus and offer you up as candy to all the women who stand on the precipice of disgrace, that they may forget their disgrace for a moment or two.

Love always,
                Your Mother, Who Loved You So Much
                    She Did Not Give Birth to You

THIRD LETTER

Somayeh,

I dedicate these pages to you: you who love pastries, who killed the man who wanted to rape your sister. You who found out you were carrying his child midway through your interrogation, then killed your unborn child. You did it because its mother had been sentenced to death. If you'd let it live, it might never have found out why.

Somayeh, I'm so close to being you. My life could have been yours, save for a few minor details. Do you remember telling us that after you had the abortion, you'd carried the foetus around with you for days in a napkin? Do you remember you said you'd committed a double murder?

Dear Somayeh, remember the last time we cried together, in a world that didn't exist? You were crouching on your bunk, down by the TV. Somayeh, I wish you could have given me some of your pain.

Somayeh, my sister, I've not once tried to forget you. Never. I've tried to preserve my love for you. I wish I could keep your last look in a napkin and carry it around with me. I wish I could breathe in your scent. I wish I could sleep next to you at night. I wish the world wasn't so painful.

Dear Somayeh, come back to me. Come, and I'll make you your chocolate cake. Come on the fourth of December, the day you were executed. Come so we can laugh at the world together, and I can entrust my child to you, in a world that doesn't exist.

My red and white and purple flower, don't forget me either, for as long as you possibly can.

Hope we meet again!

THE INTERROGATIONS have come to an end. The fish has kept growing all the while. The young woman is transferred to prison in a state of extreme agitation. Now that the fish is bigger, it'll be even harder to abort.

It was Ali Abu Nayeb who taught her how to fish.*

The first time her sister comes to visit, she tells her about the whole affair. The sister passes out. Disgrace thrums over their heads. Two days later, the young woman is called down to pick up some clothes her sister has brought for her. She does so. On the phone, her sister tells her to pick open the seam in the trousers, where she'll find the suppositories. She hopes she won't die. Ultimately, though, if the child survives, they'll all die.

---

* Ali Abu Nayeb is an ethnic Arab Iranian citizen who was interrogated and tortured at the Intelligence Ministry's detention centre in Ahvaz, where the author was also held in late 2018.

FOUR

The Diamond Stonecutter

It has to happen tonight.

She's incredulous that she's even still got the fish inside her. We've adopted the terms *fish* and *diamond* in place of *foetus* and *suppository*, because the young woman's current obsession with these terms has infected the text. Unsurprisingly, for the moment, the young woman has wiped the term *foetus* out of her mind.

It has to happen tonight. Tonight, she's got to have ... kidney stones.

But when, at what time? When the clinic is closed, for sure. When her cellmates are asleep and she can writhe in pain alone, for as long as she likes. It'll be glorious on the other side. She'll dance right out of the cell tomorrow.

The young woman takes a shower and checks herself over. She counts on her fingers. She must be three months pregnant, at least. It's definitely bigger now, and it's only going to get bigger if she leaves it in there. She glances down at her toenails, at the remnants of polish on them. She probably had them done that night, meaning the fish is the same age as the nail polish.

The closer it gets to midnight, the more confused she becomes. *It has to happen tonight.* And yet, she wants to consider how *not* to do it. Tomorrow she has to re-embark on a life without the fish. And yet, tomorrow she knows the sun is going to shine differently on the Earth. Tomorrow the sun will shine on a woman who has removed a foetus from her belly. A lonely woman in prison, a very lonely woman. Tomorrow she'll have to treat herself to a very special sweet.

It's midnight.

The young woman slides under the blanket and places a piece of diamond inside herself.

A couple of hours pass by. Nothing seems to have happened. Under the blanket, she wonders if she ought to tell her lover about all this. Would he even believe it was his?

Then, just as she asks herself the question, the pain starts – as if the foetus was waiting for it. It feels like she's being repeatedly charged at and kicked in the womb. With every kick, she shudders and bites down on the blanket, terrified that if she cries out, the others will wake up. The pain intensifies. She curses herself, the world, and everything in it. Most of all herself.

The woman in the lower bunk wakes up. 'What's up? You're moving around a lot.'

The young woman mumbles something about kidney pain, and asks for help getting out of the bunk. The bathroom seems to be miles away. With every step she wants to drop to the floor, pummel the ground and shriek, *'I can't go on!'* – but it's not the time for that. It's time to expel the creature inside her. She gets to the bathroom, shuts the door behind her and thuds her head repeatedly against the wall. The pain has broken its leash and is tearing up and down her body.

Both her friend and the night guard come to the door.

'Are you alive? Want us to call the nurse?'

'No. I don't know. I'm... constipated. No need.'

There, in the bathroom, she inserts the second diamond. She wants to go to the prayer room, but it's out of bounds at night. She's bleeding a little, and she wonders if these are clots from the month she didn't get her period. No way of knowing. The pain flares up again. The young woman rushes for the toilet. Bent double, she spreads her legs and pushes hard. The pain is excruciating. She pushes harder and harder. Finally, a foetus the size of the palm of a hand leaps out of her womb. She screams in terror.

The night guard, alerted by the noise, comes to the toilet door again.

'You alright?'

'Yep, the kidney stone came out.'

The young woman grasps the 'stone' in her fist. This is a disaster. Pain, fear, the silent hours wracked by pain, this mess, all unfolding barely ten steps away from ten CCTV cameras, each of which is overseen by a professional interrogator. They, in turn, link her to her father and brother, and so to the neighbours, and so to her friends – and perhaps, back to her cellmates. If even one them gets wind of this, what will they do to her in here?

It becomes apparent to her that she'll need to throw the foetus down the drain. Where, then, does so much fear come from? Has anybody been this fearful, ever?

Eventually she does it, but the thing doesn't so much as get past the filter. She has to crush it to pieces with the toilet brush. As she does so, she hears another scream. It's the scream of the foetus.

The young woman comes out of the toilet stall and falls to the floor, out cold. When her eyes open again, there are faces all around. For the first time, she's breathless with gratitude that in here their lives count for nothing. There are no doctors or a clinic to assess what's just happened.

But this isn't the end of the story. This could never have been the end of the story. Now she has got to live with it. For some time, the image of the foetus remains there before her eyes, and doesn't come unstuck. Now everything looks like the fish to her: her friend's signature, her cellmate's curly hair, the twisted mass of wires in the corner of the ceiling. Everything is crumpled, grasping, and screaming all the time. The judge remonstrates with her in the courtroom, and, in a fury, balls up her defence statement and throws it to the ground. She panics. The crumpled piece of paper is the foetus, and it screams. Again she faints, again she falls. Again she's dragged across the floor and the pattern on the ceramic tiles is the fish. *It can't be.* She claws at the floor. 'I can't breathe. I can't breathe. I can't breathe any more, I can't ...'

Before she crushed the foetus with the toilet brush, the young woman hadn't given much thought to the future. But the little she *had* foreseen of it was accurate. For days on end, she crouches in a corner, talks less and feels the cold more. The sun shines, but she no longer wants it. What she wants is to go to sleep, here in the dark, and never open her eyes again.

Will her lover believe any of these things, if she bothers to tell him?

Soon enough, the young woman is transferred to a different prison.

What do you do with a woman who's cold, disconsolate and haemorrhaging after a DIY abortion? *Kachi*. *Kachi* pudding is the best cure I know.

Recipe 3

Kachi pudding
for a young woman

◆ ◆ ◆

I'd asked a lot of people about the origins of *kachi* pudding before I met Anbar Nesa at Taleghani Hospital, where I'd been sent from prison for a checkup. '*Kachi* is ours,' she said, meaning the Turks. We take our hats off to them.

INGREDIENTS

1.5 litres of water
500g rock sugar
400g regular sugar
120ml rosewater
240g flour
turmeric, to taste

470ml animal-derived oil such as ghee (vegetable oil is fine, but this is better)
saffron, to taste

DIRECTIONS

Heat the water, sugar, rock sugar, saffron and rosewater until the sugar has completely dissolved. This is your syrup. Then, in a separate pan, heat the oil and add the turmeric. Add the flour, stir it in well to make a paste, and wait for it to turn pale brown. Add the syrup to the mixture, little by little. But go carefully; if you pour it in all at once, it might blow up.

They say *kachi*'s a distant cousin of *halva*, but Anbar disagrees. It ought to be much more watery, she says, and so really the recipe here is for something totally different. You can also add cumin, caraway, or coriander seeds.

◆ ◆ ◆

FIVE

The Year before the Nausea

THE YOUNG WOMAN wakes with a start. Nightmares have robbed her of meaningful sleep for three nights in a row since she arrived at this makeshift purgatory. It's a well-kept space, a hale and hearty monster. It's going to eat her alive. It's not even a house, where women might take over a corner together. It's the quarantine ward of Evin Prison.

Evin stands proudly at the edge of Tehran, marring the view of all those who pass by. The locks and chains, and the imposing iron gate, make all the more racket under torrential rain. From here, all the woman can hear is the rain pounding down. 'It's wretched,' she remarks to no one, and covers her ears with both hands.

The quarantine hall is lined with row upon row of double beds, most of which are unoccupied. It must be 200 metres long, at least. The young woman gazes up at the ceiling. It's covered with cameras, some very close to her. They are recording the young woman from every angle: from north, south, east, west, southwest, southeast. They'll capture her waking with a start, her fitful pacing up and down, her facing the wall hunched up, her sliding under the blanket, her coming out from under the blanket, her filling a glass of water, her drinking the water, her going to the toilet, her pissing, her watching TV, her constant gazing at the ceiling and her counting the cameras. Needless to say, she mustn't do anything she's not allowed to do. Unless it's under the blanket.

The young woman turns the TV volume up full blast, to drown out sound of the rain. Putting her fingers in her ears was never going to be sustainable. The noise is unbearable, but she does want to watch the programme.

They returned her, in a state of desolation, to Evin Prison. Covid-19 is everywhere and the new health protocols require that she spend fourteen days in quarantine before being transferred to the common ward. Fourteen days in isolation feels all right. For a while she can be by herself, and hear no other voices.

New arrivals to Evin Prison enter the quarantine ward via a huge metal door. Then there's a turnstile, then the hall itself, and the thicket of double bunk beds. No virus could possibly escape this place. They've even closed the windows and hung up some acrylic sheets. There are two washbasins, and a third sink in the kitchen. The young woman has inspected them, one by one.

Lying on the bed now, she thinks about the past. These days, the young woman is equipped to endure any amount of empty time. Anything that enters her mind gets chewed over a thousand times. Repetition is her habit and her survival mechanism. Out there on the ward opposite, life might be going on as normal, with dancing, birthday celebrations, even singing. But this only makes her smile. *Good for them, having something to sing about.*

For now, she still has the right to exercise for two hours in the prison yard, twice a day. The inmates in the opposite yard have to be cleared out before she can head out – she's potentially infectious after all. Sometimes, in transit, she can see the women whose singing and dancing have kept her smile alive. *Greetings, you strangers, stars of this dark night! Greetings, you life-saving women!*

The fresh air and sunlight ought to invigorate her, especially as the quarantine ward is always too dark. But all she ever really wants to do is get back into bed and keep brooding over the past, and she always does so as quickly as she can.

In a sense, she's glad the earlier misfortunes are behind her. She gets up, walks around the empty ward, and looks at the walls. A large mural has been painted on one of them: a crayon landscape featuring an evergreen tree, with a river, the sun above and a house. It's signed: azar. i love you.

The mural has been crafted with particular care. Its greens are very green, its blues a deep, deep blue. The woman is a child of a river herself, and she devours the colour. It turns her belly into a blue sea, where the fish live. 'Azar, I love you, who painted this so well,' she says to the empty room. 'I love you, Azar, who painted the river in such a way that it cuts through the prison walls. Out towards the Karun and Aras rivers and Lake Zrebar. I long for the blues of your sky and rivers. Azar, I love you, a woman I don't know.'

The woman thinks about Azar and the others who were here before her. It's still the early days of Covid-19, and this hall has only just been designated as a quarantine ward. Anyone here previously was here for other purposes. They'd been held long enough to acquire crayons and transform the wall into a river. Azar I-Love-You was just one of them.

The other walls are covered with crooked lines – colourful ones, but still. Between a battered rice cooker and switched-off refrigerators covered with dust, it looks as if a second 'Azar' – shorter perhaps, not so tidy – has pissed over the walls a little above ground level, while a compatriot of hers drew a new sky under the ceiling. Walking from column to column, the young woman finds 'Saba', who, in clear, polished handwriting, has written lines of poetry all along the walls. Based on their content, Saba was very much in love, and probably quite young as well. She must have held herself in high regard, because she wrote absolutely everywhere, inserted her own name repeatedly in the blank spaces, and used the walls to doodle on as well. While clearly literate, Saba hasn't written any poems to the young woman's liking. She was a philistine.

Just a little above the painting, signed 'azar. i love you', Saba has written the following:

One: Buried beside each teardrop of mine are thousands of memories / So many memories have I, they seem to cover a century / My throat is burning because of a love like Venus's / But when there is no love, it cannot go on.

     Saba, Thursday, 6 September, 2018

Two: Unveil yourself, I am your lover / I am in love, in love with your beauty spot / Whenever I see anybody who bids for a vision of you / I bid for your bidder.

Three: Lean on my shoulder, my lotus flower / So I won't see in your eyes the sorrow of having nothing to lean on.

Four: A blue ceiling I want to build, with blue windows / I want a moonlit night, for me and you.

The woman is reading the poems in mid-2020, but Saba wrote them in this airless hall in mid-2018. To this day, the young women doesn't know anything else about Azar or Saba, or the others who were kept here, and has no idea why they were separated from the women in the yard opposite. In all likelihood, they, too, went on to face ever more doors, more walls.

Other poems written by Saba run as follows:

Any direction I go in, the way is closed / Someone has locked up my luck with a spell / A mountain of unease I carry on my shoulder / My spirit hangs by a thread these days.

Oh, my heart, pin your hopes no more on freedom / A lion is a prisoner when it loves a gazelle / Sorrow has caused a commotion in my heart / In the midst of this tumult, the lump in my throat stops me crying / I wear my enemy on my head like a crown / When my love holds a dagger by my side / He broke his pact with me, the one who loved him / But my heart remains faithful to its pact with him.

The young woman begins to doze off. All too soon, she's jolted awake by the scream of a woman she later learns is called 'Hengameh'.

'I have been in quarantine for twenty-one days!' Hengameh bawls. 'This is an injustice!'

The ward overseer responds calmly: 'It's for your own sake. Quarantine is the opposite of an injustice; it's for all of our protection. If somebody new arrives, the quarantine is extended. It's just your luck. It's got nothing to do with justice.'

Hengameh screams again and continues to babble away on the same theme. The way she talks would make the crayon tree shed its leaves, never mind what it's doing to the inmates. The young woman tries to go back to sleep, but can't. Twenty-one days is nothing. Why are people so difficult?

There are other notes on the walls, which, taken together, might shed some light on what kind of a place this used to be. On the first column to her left, someone has written:

Started sentence: Sept. 3, 2017
Sentence length: 3 years
Release date: God knows
Aug. 27, 2020: One more year

A series of dates are also scribbled down there:

THE YEAR BEFORE THE NAUSEA

27/8, one month
28/8, two months
29/8, three months
30/8, four months
31/9, five months
1/9, six months
2/9, seven months
22/8/20 23/8/20 24/8/23 25/8/20 26/8/20
27/8/20 Freedom, God willing.

There must have been something substantially different about these women compared to the women in the ward opposite. The current incumbents are here because they may or may not be carrying Covid-19, but what marked out Azar, Saba and the rest of their cellmates will always be unclear.

The young woman holds imaginary stars in her hand, which come to her on dark nights like this. *Stars like these are in almost everybody's life*, she likes to think. They're very bright, but only really shine once the darkness has enveloped her. Then they become visible. The woman puts each and every one of them into her hand and closes it, and a pool of light gathers under her fingernails. The stars sometimes smell like caraway, sometimes like fish, sometimes like the air-conditioning at home in midsummer. Sometimes the stars have drunk Arabic coffee, and when they open their mouths, the scent is intoxicating. These are the stars that rescue a person from a never-ending state of suffering, like three years spent in a room without any light, which in truth *is* intolerable for even twenty-one days. The stars go for the ears, the hands, the hair, finally the lips and the heart. Then they start life all over again. They open the concrete wall out towards a blue lake. The stars grin at the cracks and turn into love poems on the walls.

SIX

And Now for the Shadow-Puppet Show

THE SHADOWS OF SIXTEEN WOMEN and eight children are lined up on the wall. The young woman sees them and jerks around, but there's nobody else there with her. *How can this be?* she tries to ask, and discovers that she can't speak.

They can't just massacre twenty-four women and children yards away from the dancing women of Ward 1, can they? This isn't the Anfal.* In any event, how is it possible for their shadows to be there, but not the women and children themselves? Of course it's possible. There were sixteen women and eight children here; none of them had a name, and they've drawn the shadows of their homes and their outlines on the wall. *That must be it. Perhaps.*

---

* The Anfal ('Spoils of War') campaign was a counterinsurgency operation launched by Saddam Hussein at the end of the Iran–Iraq War in 1988 to eliminate Kurdish rebel groups; tens of thousands of Kurds were massacred.

The shadows are plainly women because their hair, their scarves, and sometimes their skirts are clearly discernible, and they're taller. The children accompanying them are taller than any adults the young woman has ever seen, but they are clearly children with their mothers. They are children because they've drawn crooked lines all along the walls, 20 centimetres above the floor. They are children because they've left their shoes behind. By turns their mothers hold them in their arms, breastfeed them, and hold their hands. Sixteen women and eight children, lined up on the wall.

Sound is added to the shadow-puppet theatre now, but nobody utters a word. It's the sound of water, waves, splashing feet, the wind, people wailing. The woman tries to isolate each sound, tries to ascribe each one to a given shadow as best she can, and shuts her eyes so as to remember them better as they are. It won't be long before the sun comes up or a candle is lit and it all stops. In her mind's eye, the shadows move together but are released one by one; each comes forward as an individual, alone or with a child in tow. She tries to establish how each woman sounds, how she smells.

AND NOW FOR THE SHADOW-PUPPET SHOW

The first woman dances a waltz, exquisitely and passionately. The sound of the wind accompanies her. She whisks her hair from side to side like the branches of an oak tree. First she dances with one child, then with another. Her pleated skirt fans out in the wind as she twirls in place, so quickly and so precisely that the children pull back little by little. Alone in the frame, the woman keeps dancing, her gaze fixed on the youngsters as they exit. The only thing that belongs to this curly-headed woman is the sound of the wind. It challenges her to dance, but it cannot defeat her. The young woman is amazed by her skill. The harder the wind blows, the more beautifully the shadow dances. She's all the more adept now that the children are gone. They are safe and won't be caught in the storm, but she will be – willingly – as will the scent of daffodils. This is the shadow of Narges Mohammadi.*

---

* Narges Mohammadi, a life-long campaigner for human rights in Iran, has faced repeated incarceration in her country of birth and documented the abuses meted out to her, and to others. Her book, *White Torture*, about the practice of solitary confinement, was published in Persian in 2020 and in English in 2022. In October 2023, while in prison, she was awarded the Nobel Peace Prize. Her husband, Taghi Rahmani, and their children, Ali and Kiana, reside in Paris.

Recipe 4

Pumpkin pie
for Narges Mohammadi

◆ ◆ ◆

INGREDIENTS FOR THE PIE CRUST

250g flour   ¼ tsp salt
330g sugar   1 egg
185g butter   60ml cold water

DIRECTIONS

Rub together the butter and the flour until the mixture has the consistency of breadcrumbs. Then add the salt and sugar. Now whisk the egg and cold water together in a separate bowl. Add this to the mixture. Then knead it until the dough comes together as a single ball. If it sticks to your hand, add a little flour to solve the problem.

Leave the dough to chill in the refrigerator for 40 minutes. Then roll it out to your desired thickness. Once ready, place the dough into a pie tin.

INGREDIENTS FOR THE PUMPKIN PIE FILLING

390g condensed milk   ¼ tsp salt
2 eggs   1 tsp cinnamon
½ tsp ground ginger   600g pumpkin
½ tsp nutmeg powder   purée

DIRECTIONS

Preheat the oven to 180°C. Mix the ingredients thoroughly, and pour the filling into the pie tin. Bake for around one hour.

Now put a bouquet of daffodils* on the table, brew some tea and enjoy!

◆ ◆ ◆

---

* This is a pun on the name Narges, which is the Persian name for the *narcissus* plant family, which includes daffodils.

THE WALL SUDDENLY turns dark. Pitch-black. But the sounds carry on. Then a tiny circle of light appears to one side. It's a woman, seated, immobile and inscrutable. No information can be gleaned about her from her appearance. She just sits there, raising her hands to the sky. Then she drops one hand down to her breast, and squeezes it, spraying milk across the wall. The young woman has seen this before, and knows what's going on: a woman is relieving her breasts of milk in the dead of the night. Her body language makes it clear how painful this is.

The young woman without a shadow suddenly knows who this woman with a shadow is. None of the eight children are hers. This woman's shadow is fainter than the others, and as each jet of milk issues from her breast, she becomes fainter still. When the milk runs out, she disappears altogether. The young woman calls out to her: 'Makieh! Makieh! Makieh!' But it's too late. The wall has gone dark again.

Recipe 5

Gosh-e fil ('Elephant ears') *for Makieh*

◆ ◆ ◆

You must make *gosh-e fil* on Saturdays because we make it on Saturdays. You can cook a lot of *gosh-e fil* with 1 kilogram of flour. And so our Sundays, when we can receive visitors, become very sweet, because everybody brings *gosh-e fils* to the visitors' room. Whip up some *gosh-e fils* whenever you need *a lot* of pastries. It's not at all messy and is impossible to get wrong. You don't even need an oven. The sweetness is up to you. You can make it very, very sweet or you can choose to be more restrained. Its shape is also your choice – square, triangular or resembling an elephant's ear. All work. Niloufar likes it square and Sepideh Kashani likes the shape of an elephant's ear because she has something like an elephant in her.

INGREDIENTS FOR THE DOUGH

5 eggs
240g yoghurt
150g cornflour
1kg flour

1 tbsp baking powder
½ tsp baking soda
150g oil

DIRECTIONS

Put five eggs into a mixer or bowl and whisk them thoroughly. Add the yoghurt to the egg mixture.

Add baking powder to the mix – stir until it's fluffy. Then add the cornflour, the oil and the baking soda to the yoghurt, one after the other. Mix well. Now add the flour and knead it thoroughly until the dough's texture is consistent. Then cover the bowl and let the dough rest for an hour. Then we roll out the dough and cut out the shapes we want – your *gosh-e fil* can be whatever size you want, and however thick you want. The thinner you roll the dough out, the crispier your *gosh-e fil* will be. Fry the pieces well and dip them into the syrup.

INGREDIENTS FOR THE SYRUP

1 cup water	saffron and cardamom
1 cup sugar	powder to taste

DIRECTIONS

Heat the water and sugar together until the sugar has dissolved, then add the saffron and cardamom. The sweetness of the *gosh-e fil* hinges on how long you leave your pastries in the syrup – one minute, two minutes, ten minutes ... And they can be as sweet as you like!

◆ ◆ ◆

AND NOW FOR THE SHADOW-PUPPET SHOW

THE NEXT WOMAN WALKS gently in high heels. She has a straight posture, very smooth hair, and a child in her arms, whom she sets down on the floor. She hands the youngster what looks like a bundle of pencils or ballpoint pens. Together, they draw on the walls: one on this side, the other on that. The woman in heels draws a sea, and her little child sketches in waves. Then the woman draws waves, too, and the child draws fish. The child draws the wind, and together they raise the sea level higher and higher. A storm is gathering. The waves begin to dance. The sound of the waves is the sound of their shoes.

The woman and her child aren't trapped, but they are struggling. The mother's hair is long; the child's tresses are not, yet, but she's as strong as her mother. They scramble to reach one another in the roiling sea. The woman throws her hair out to her daughter, and the girl throws back her own. Treading water, they bind themselves together using their hair like rope. The waves have separated them from each other's reach, but their hair keeps them bonded, no matter the distance. The mother and child are Nazanin Zaghari-Ratcliffe and her daughter Gabriella, also called 'Gisou', which means 'tresses' in Persian.* Their sound is the sound of the stormy sea, the waves that part them.

---

* Nazanin Zaghari-Ratcliffe is a British-Iranian dual national and journalist. She was detained in Iran on 3 April 2016, and only finally released on 16 March 2022. It is not possible to reproduce exactly the play on words in the author's original text.

Recipe 6

Scones
for Nazanin

◆ ◆ ◆

'From each of her fingers, a talent rains.' So goes the Persian saying, and it's praise that Nazanin Zaghari-Ratcliffe rightfully deserves. Really, from each of her fingers, *twenty* talents rain, because Nazanin is a master of at least 200 skills. Besides tailoring, painting and 197 other things, she's a fine baker with a unique touch and remarkable attention to detail. I still remember the sight of her standing next to the table in Room 1, in a brownish apron, baking ginger cookies for her lovely daughter, Gisou. This was where we became friends. Though the time we had together was short, such was her glow that the smell of ginger and cinnamon still reminds me of her, and of her ardent wait to meet her little Gisou again. Nazanin was very aware of the quantity of sugar in her baking, and always took care not to put in too much. She also loved cinnamon. These simple scones are presented in honour of her, and our memories of her.

Making scones is quick and easy. I use date syrup instead of sugar; you can do the same or use honey, especially if you're on a diet or – like Nazanin – you want the number on the scales not to budge. These take less than 10 minutes to make, and you can bring them to the breakfast table in under a half-hour. Offer them hot to your dear daughter, who mustn't be late for school.

INGREDIENTS

250g flour
50g butter, softened
30g date syrup, honey, or sugar
2 eggs
1 tsp baking powder

as much cinnamon as you fancy
crushed walnuts and seedless raisins, depending on your budget

DIRECTIONS

Beat the eggs, add the date syrup and add the flour and baking powder into the mix. Add the butter and stir until the dough acquires a uniform texture. Then add the cinnamon, crushed walnuts or raisins if you're using them. Roll out the dough with a rolling pin or your palms so it's 2.5cm thick. Cut out your scones with a round cutter and place them in a 180°C oven for 10–15 minutes, until the tops rise and the bottoms turn golden. To improve the colour, you can also brush the top with an egg wash (and saffron!) before baking.

◆ ◆ ◆

AND NOW FOR THE SHADOW-PUPPET SHOW

THE YOUNG WOMAN WONDERS: would she, too, have had a shadow on the wall if she hadn't ended her pregnancy? What else might her shadow reveal about her character?

The next shadow is very tall – so tall, in fact, that her head extends outside the frame. But she's definitely a woman, with a prominent chest, carrying a load on her shoulders that is heavier than she is. For three days and three nights, it snows incessantly. The shadow disappears when the new day dawns, and reappears when darkness falls, trudging on but never quite reaching the edge of the frame. The road has no end. The snow piles up around this shadow-*kolbar*, ankle-deep. If it goes on like this, she'll collapse here on the mountainside. The young woman knows this woman has a child of her own. In a few moments, all this suffering – set against the backdrop of the Kurdish song 'Sweet Is My Sweet' (Shirin Shirin) – will end. The woman with the frozen ankles comes to a halt. She remains unmoving on the spot for three more days and three more nights. The snowfall lasts for so long that it completely covers the body of Mahin Boland Karami.

The next shadow arrives.

This shadow has wings, which she's using to cover up a child. *If I were that shadow,* the young woman thinks, *I'd be flying out of here the first chance I had. Why doesn't she fly?* Then the shadow gets to her feet, and in so doing reveals that her ankles are chained. But Elaheh Darvishi's shadow is tireless.* She walks left and right, this way and that. Then she runs as far as the chain will allow, turns and runs in the other direction. She never gives up the bid for freedom. The child with her is her son, Ibrahim or, as she is forced to call him, Ali.†

---

* Elaheh Darvishi was arrested when her husband was accused of participating in the terrorist attack on the Ahvaz military parade on 22 September 2018, in which five gunmen shot at the parade commemorating Sacred Defence Week.
† Ethnic Arabs are singled out for persecution in Iran's prisons, and are denigrated for being Sunni Muslim rather than Shi'i. Elaheh was made to name her child Ali, after Prophet Muhammad's son-in-law, whom Shi'is consider the first Imam, instead of Ibrahim.

Recipe 7

Doughnuts with crème pâtissière for Elaheh Darvishi

◆ ◆ ◆

See the world, now, through the eyes of a woman who crosses the hallway ever so slowly, so that she doesn't fall. While walking, she laughs and places her hand on her big, bulging belly. She tries to control her expression, and says: 'It's kicking.' Today, all life is the smile of this pregnant eighteen-year-old woman. She's carrying all the pain of the world in there, but still, it makes her laugh. She returns to the ward and takes the hand of her friend, who is not a baker.

'Right. Now I have a craving for a cream-filled *piroshki*. What do you classy people call it? *Doneh*? *Dona*?'

'Doughnut?'

'Yes, yes, doughnut. I am prepared to give everything I have for a doughnut.' Then she rolls her eyes, which are as big as her belly, and her tongue passes over her lips.

INGREDIENTS

500g flour	1 tsp baking powder
450g sugar	1 tsp salt
60g butter	120ml milk
2 eggs	60ml lukewarm water

DIRECTIONS

There's no need for an oven to make doughnuts. A gas stove and vegetable oil will do. But the dough has to be made fresh. Before doing anything, you've got to wash your hands thoroughly. And don't forget to wear a flowery dress.

Mix the baking powder, salt and lukewarm water together in a glass. Cover and let them have a *tête-à-tête* for 15 minutes. Rub the flour and the butter together thoroughly, until the dough has a uniform consistency. Add the sugar and the two eggs, and knead it, so it's ready to drink some milk just like Elaheh's baby. Add the milk and keep kneading. Add the baking powder mix. If the dough starts sticking to your hand, add a little more flour. When I'm nervous, I pound it with my palm. It calms us both down. Then grease a dish with cooking oil, pour the dough in, cover it with cellophane, and keep it somewhere warm for an hour and a half. The warmer the spot, the better it'll rise. It's not a bad idea to cover the dish with a blanket as well.

Now grease a tray, cut the dough into any shapes and sizes you fancy, and place them on it. Make a well in the middle of each doughnut with a flour-coated knife. Cover the doughnuts with a clean cloth, let them rest for another 10 minutes and then fry them in very hot oil. After that, you can fill them with *crème pâtissière*.

CRÈME PÂT' INGREDIENTS

400ml milk
20g cornflour
4 large egg yolks

40g butter
125g sugar
20g flour

DIRECTIONS

First, start to warm the milk in a pan. In another container, mix the egg yolks with the sugar, and add the flour. Add the essential cornflour right at the end. When the milk is close to the boiling point, take it off the heat and stir it in with the rest. Put the whole lot on a low flame, stirring continuously until thickened. Now it's time to take the cream off the heat. Keep stirring. The pot might whinge that it misses the heat – don't we all – but persevere and make it understand. Now, gently, add the butter. Continue stirring until it's happily absorbed.

Elaheh was rebellious, and uncannily cute as she ambled down the corridors of death with a child in her belly. She was a short, pale-skinned woman with big hazel eyes, who loved painting and cooking. She'd sketch the soil and breastfed her baby under bullets and rockets, laughing all the while. She turned nineteen around the time her son Ibrahim was born; they made her call him 'Ali'. She was a goddess in mourning for her youth and her life.

◆ ◆ ◆

THE NEXT SHADOW IS LOST. She's kneeling on the floor and seems to be looking for something as well as signalling to someone, jabbing a forefinger repeatedly at something out of the frame. She pounds the ground in frustration and points her finger again. Then, all of a sudden, she's set upon by a group of men. They beat her with cables and break the offending finger. The woman seems to know what's going to happen, and tries to launch herself out of the frame into the arms of the shadows.

'No!' she cries out plaintively. 'This isn't right!' It means nothing to her attackers. This shadow belongs to Zahra Hosseini. 'For just one minute,' she entreats them. 'For just one minute, for God's sake, let me see my children!'

The young woman wants to tell the shadow-men that they've got it wrong, that the pointed finger doesn't mean what they think it means. All the shadow wants is to see her girls, Esra and Sana. But it's not within their capacity to understand.*

---

* The respective fates of several of the women named in this chapter are not known, beyond the detail Sepideh has provided here. In an earlier collection of her prison-diary fragments, *Tilapia Sucks the Blood of Hur Al-Azim* (2020), Zahra Hosseini is described as an ethnic Arab who was accused – without evidence – of spying for ISIS, alongside Makieh Neisi.

Recipe 8

*Lemon meringue pie
for Zahra Hosseini*

◆ ◆ ◆

Zahra Hosseini, born in 1995, has black eyebrows and long, curly black hair. After she was forced by her family to get married at the age of eighteen, she had two daughters, Esra and Zana. She moved straight from one man's home to the next, and never tasted freedom. Zahra was also made always to wear a veil outside. Once, she whispered in my ear: 'When we're released, let's go together to the banks of the Karun River, let our hair down, and dance.'

We once saw a picture of this dessert in a magazine. 'I don't know what that is, but I want it,' she said.

Bake this lemon meringue pie today, right this minute, after you've sung 'Winter Is Over' (*Sar Oomad Zemestoon*).* As Zahra said at the time, it looks perfect, and I can assure you it tastes heavenly as well. What more do you want?

---

* 'Winter is Over' is a popular Iranian protest song. It was written by the radical Saeed Soltanpour, a member of the Organisation of Iranian People's Fedai Guerrillas, in the early 1970s. It became popular during the 1979 Revolution, and was sung once again on the streets during the 2009 Green Movement protests. Saeed Soltanpour was executed by the Islamic Republic in 1981.

PIE BASE INGREDIENTS

200g flour
70g icing sugar
a tiny bit of salt
125g butter
1 egg

4 drops vanilla extract, or the tip of a teaspoonful of the real thing

DIRECTIONS

Cream together the butter, icing sugar and vanilla extract, then add the beaten egg, flour and salt. Knead it until you've got a smooth dough. Put in the refrigerator for 40 minutes, then take out, flatten with a rolling pin or your hands, and press into a tart or pie tin of your choosing. Prick small holes in the surface of the dough with a fork. Cover with greaseproof paper, pour a fistful of dried chickpeas or dried beans over the top, and spread them about (this is to stop the dough from burning). Put in the oven at 180°C for 15 minutes. Take it out, remove the chickpeas and put back in for 10 more minutes. Now for the lemon curd.

LEMON CURD INGREDIENTS

3 eggs
100g sugar
zest of 1 large lime
80ml fresh lemon juice
30g butter

3g gelatin
3 tbsp cream cheese
as much chopped fresh mint as you fancy

DIRECTIONS

Mix the beaten eggs, sugar, lemon juice and cream cheese together. Stir really well for 10–15 minutes on a low heat. Pour the gelatin into cold water to soak. When it's softened well, drain the water and add the gelatin to the mixture while it's still warm, so the gelatin can melt. Then let it cool down. Once that's done, add the chopped mint, lime zest and butter. Pour into the tin and put in the refrigerator to set. And now for the meringue.

ITALIAN MERINGUE INGREDIENTS

3 medium egg whites   70ml water
200g sugar

DIRECTIONS

Pour the egg whites into a bowl. Put the sugar and water into a bain-marie and put it on the stove. Use a sugar thermometer to monitor the heat (you're looking for 125°C). In the meantime, use an electric whisk to whip the egg whites into stiff peaks. When the sugar-water hits 125°, drizzle thinly over the cloud of egg whites while stirring continuously. Keep stirring for 10 minutes until it all cools down. Take the tart out of the fridge and use a funnel to decorate the top with the meringue. If you've got a blowtorch, use it to turn the top a deep golden colour.

◆ ◆ ◆

The young woman has been facing the wall since the beginning of winter. The shadow-puppet show began on the 22 December, and for six days and six nights, she's watched the weighed-down form of Mahin Boland Karami crossing and then falling victim to the snowy mountain. Makieh's shadow didn't last long at all. Neither did Zahra Hosseini's. Nazanin's shadow lasted only as long as the storm, and Narges's danced for just a few, triumphant hours. It must still have been 28 December when Narges finished; starting then, another shadow appears on the wall. It has long, untidy hair, squats in the corner of the frame, and does not move. This woman spends four hundred horrifying days next to the wall. Her eyes are fixed on an unknown spot. It seems reasonable to infer that there was a child involved here, too. But her wait for this child is permeated with a different kind of silence.

Seasons cycle by. The snow melts and the sun bursts out of hiding, warming the trunks of the oak trees on the walls of Ward 2 of Evin Prison, the leaves of which turn green once more. But the shadow on the wall either doesn't know about this, or doesn't care. She doesn't care about the wildfires that have ripped through Kurdistan, as the sun now burns. She's been consumed by something more painful to her and to her alone. When the child arrives at the close of those four hundred days, she leaps up and runs towards it, only to find there's something in her way: a glass barrier. The young woman wants to write down every one of those four hundred days. She wants to put every moment of Maryam Haji-Hosseini's silence into words.*

---

* Maryam Haji-Hosseini is a distinguished Iranian scientist and inventor. She was arrested on 'espionage' charges in 2019 and held in solitary confinement for a total of 412 days before being sentenced to ten years in prison. She was denied furlough during Covid-19.

Recipe 9

Dutch cheesecake
for Maryam Haji-Hosseini

◆ ◆ ◆

Maryam is in the kitchen every morning mixing ingredients, fast as lightning, for all the dishes and pastries she wants to make that day. She has a fixed recipe for every one of them. The Iranian meatball dish called *kotlet*, for example, is 'Noodles plus meat. Onions. Potatoes. Raisins. The kitchen sink. Gasoline. Nuts, bolts, other toppings.' The ingredients for her cheesecake are as follows: 'Digestive biscuits. Clotted cream. Cow bones. Two metric tons of gelatin.'

It's as if she has yet to accept that she's in prison. If a prison official comes onto the ward, she'll inevitably invite him to execute her. She gets up early every morning without fail to study and learn before setting aside a little time for her peerless cooking. Baking is a more recent pursuit, but she's so extraordinary at it that I can't do her justice, even though she only allocates five minutes a day to it, so it doesn't eat into her study time. Her daily schedule over ten years in prison is as follows: twenty-one and a half hours of reading books, one hour of sleep, fifty-five minutes of asking to be executed, half an hour of calisthenics and five minutes of cooking and baking.

As such, even as we – the rest of the baking community – raise grievances against Maryam Haji-Hosseini, both for insulting the cheesecake and wounding our prideful hearts, we also offer her the best cheesecake in the world as a token of our appreciation.

BASE INGREDIENTS

300g flour
1 tsp vanilla
2 tsp yoghurt
140g butter or
   shortening

1 egg
1 tsp honey
2 tbsp milk powder
120g icing sugar

DIRECTIONS

Mix the flour and the shortening together to get the dough started. Then mix in the other ingredients using an electric whisk or your hands, and knead again to make a smooth dough (add flour to your hands if it sticks). Then put in the refrigerator to firm up. In the meantime, make the cream filling.

FILLING INGREDIENTS

2 eggs
300g cream cheese
200g yoghurt
200g clotted cream

100g sugar
3 tbsp *crème pâtissière*
   (see p. 93)
1 tbsp flour

DIRECTIONS

Mix all the ingredients together and stir. Now take the dough out of the refrigerator and spread out in your tart or pie tin. Use a fork to poke little holes on the surface. Then pour the cream onto it, and put in an oven at 150°C for 40 minutes, give or take. It'll be ready when the surface turns golden. Take it out and decorate it with more *crème pât'* or fruit.

◆ ◆ ◆

THE NEXT SHADOW begins as a lone child. Every day for three years, when it wakes up in the morning, it gets a little bit taller. It gets taller each time it waits in line for food, for the roll call, or for a visitation. It has to grow tall, or it'll be squashed. Each time it stands in line to hear the names of those on death row, it gets taller. Between each round of lashes and humiliation, it gets taller. Finally it assumes the shadow of an adult woman. Prison is her only frame. She has a child of her own, somewhere, and each and every one of her family members is imprisoned in a different frame. She's never forgotten how to love. The woman raises a finger and draws a heart in the air, as if she knows she's being watched. She smiles.

This is the shadow of Fatima Muthanna.* Gradually, though, Fatima's shadow begins to crumple into herself and grow smaller again, as if shrivelling up from pain. Eventually, she dwindles away to a trailing half-presence, like the lost end of a skein of wool. Another woman enters the frame, picks her up and starts knitting.

---

* Fatima Muthanna is a political detainee in her fifties. She was first imprisoned together with her mother, a member of the political-militant opposition group the People's Mojahedin Organisation, when she was just three years old. She is currently serving a fifteen-year sentence.

Recipe 10

Date crumble
for Fatima Muthanna

♦ ♦ ♦

Fatima's husband Mr Hasan is a baker, and she's very much in love with him, so this one's suffused with anxiety. We've got to make her something 'warming' due to her intestinal trouble. She sees everything in terms of whether it's 'warming' or 'chilling', up to and including her friendships. She only makes friends with the warm people. But fortunately there's an easy fix for everything: rock candy. Like so:

'Fatima! Sour cherry jam. Is it warming or chilling?'
'Chilling.'
'Damn. What can we do?'
'Add a piece of rock candy while you're making it!'
Or: 'Fatima! It's cold outside. Don't go out.'
'Relax. I'll wear my rock candy overcoat. That'll solve it.'

We get hold of dates grown in the very warmest regions and we turn them into a date crumble, in the vain hope it'll get her to give up rock candy once and for all. Fatima's new cure-all goes like this:

BASE INGREDIENTS

600g flour
1 tsp vanilla
280g butter or shortening

50g cream
1 egg
50g golden syrup
2 tbsp milk powder

DIRECTIONS

Blend all the ingredients together into a smooth dough and put in the refrigerator to chill. Prepare the filling.

FILLING INGREDIENTS

500g dates	powdered cardamom
200g flour	and cinnamon,
200g oil	to taste

DIRECTIONS

Mix the flour and oil together, and heat them slowly on the stove. Squish the dates thoroughly with a meat tenderiser or similar, into as much of a paste as you can. Add this to the pot, then add the spices. Turn off the heat and let it cool completely.

Cut the dough you made earlier in half. Put one half in the freezer, and use the other half to line a 20cm × 30cm cake tin; spoon the filling over the latter. When the other half of the dough is frozen, take it out and grate it over the top. Put the tin in a 180°C oven and bake. When it's done, you can use the grill to turn the top half golden.

◆ ◆ ◆

AND NOW FOR THE SHADOW-PUPPET SHOW

THE SHADOW-SKEIN'S FAMILY has been executed. Its children are outside the frame. They love one another very much. The second shadow casts the yarn onto a knitting needle and makes an initial row of one, two, three, four, five, two hundred and twenty stitches. Then it starts on the second row, and on and on it goes, knitting continuously for eight years without once looking up or asking Heaven for anything. Eight years is the length of time the skein has spent in prison before assuming its current form. The shadow-woman knits the skein into a colossal muffler. She doesn't once complain about the pain.

The shadows within the frame belong to mothers whose children have been taken away from them. That much is clear. The shadow woman has borne witness to the mothers, to their restlessness, crouching and pleading. For ten years now, this has been her life too. But the young woman is transfixed by her, because she refuses to protest. She ignores the edges of the frame and focuses fully on the task at hand. Mahin's shadow may stand tall now. By taking stock of Fatima Muthanna's pain, the knitting shadow ends up with a muffler long enough to cover the necks of all the children of the world. It's Zahra Zehtabchi to whose shadow they're indebted.*

---

* Zahra Zehtabchi, a sociologist and social scientist, was jailed for nearly ten years in 2014 for 'armed insurrection against the regime' and 'war against God'.

Recipe 11

Saffron cookies for Zahra Zehtabchi

◆ ◆ ◆

One of Zahra Zehtabchi's distinguishing characteristics is her simplicity. Another is her absolute conviction that saffron must not be boiled. Out of respect for the latter, we'll try to avoid doing that here.

INGREDIENTS

250g flour	cardamom powder
165g butter	1 tsp saffron
the tip of a teaspoonful of vanilla or	2 egg yolks
	70g sugar

DIRECTIONS

Cream the sugar, butter and vanilla. Add the beaten egg yolks and the flour and mix. Finally, add the saffron. Cut into cookies and bake at 180°C for 10 minutes.

◆ ◆ ◆

IN DECEMBER 2021, twelve years after the young woman first encountered fifteen of the shadows and after six of them had been taken away, the sixteenth shadow finally arrives.* It belongs to Paulina Salas. It's a cold night, and parts of the hills beyond the window, she can see, are covered with snow. But the shadow is ablaze with warmth. All sounds seem to emanate

---

* *The author writes*: For reasons unknown, six of the shadows didn't make it into the show, although they'd been part of the company since the spirited Maryam Akbari Monfared entered the frame. Their faces look exactly alike, and their particulars have been lost for the purposes of the play. But in a letter to her lover – a thirteen-year-long story of shadows – the young woman had included the names of Sakineh Sagoori, Azita Rafieezadeh, Elham Barmaki and Kobra Behyari, and also referred to two other unnamed Kurdish women. We'll have to be content with this for now. Perhaps one day they'll occupy a stage of their own. So many names have been lost to us forever; others may only be biding their time. What is indisputable is that there's at least one young woman in prison who carries all these names in her bosom, and their images, too, like the image of Shirin Alam Hooli's slippers as she ran towards the gallows. We are still running with her.

Editorial note: Sakineh Sagoori, like Elaheh Darvishi, was arrested and imprisoned after the attack on the Ahvaz military parade. Sakineh's husband had died in Syria. Azita Rafieezadeh and her husband were imprisoned for four years for teaching at the Bahá'í Institute for Higher Education. Elham Barmaki, a dual Iranian-Cypriot citizen, was arrested on August 2011 on charges of 'espionage' and experienced fourteen months of solitary confinement before being transferred to the women's ward of Evin Prison. We find out more about Kobra Behyari in Chapter Eleven.

AND NOW FOR THE SHADOW-PUPPET SHOW

from her: uproarious laughter, shouts of 'Death to the dictator!' and, yes, weeping, too. Paulina Salas enters the frame and coaxes each and every one of the shadows back out to join her. Even the shadows the young woman has never seen make themselves known: Gisou, Kiana, Alireza. Paulina's mouth opens wide in a shout, her hands rise up to the sky, and the movements of her mouth are aped by the mouths of the shadow-children who haven't yet learned to speak. When her shadow walks, they all walk behind her, each in her own style, sometimes dancing, sometimes bent double, sometimes blinded by tears. Together, they are abolishing the night. 'Paulina Salas' is Maryam Akbari Monfared, the young mother of young detainees.*

---

* Maryam Akbari Monfared is a member of the People's Mojahedin Organisation and a long-time prisoner of conscience. She was arrested in 2009 and sentenced to fifteen years in prison for 'war against God'. At the time of writing, she has yet to be granted a single day of furlough. In March 2021, she was exiled to Semnan Prison.

SEVEN
Paulina Salas

THE YOUNG WOMAN enters the common ward after fourteen days, and sees Paulina Salas.*

'Hello! I'm Paulina Salas.'

'Hello there. I am a young woman.'

'Pleased to meet you. I'm a young woman, too.'

The young woman leaves Paulina Salas and makes a beeline for the library, which is decently stocked. She chooses a book and takes it back to her bunk. Three days pass before she's able to read any of it – she hardly has a moment to herself in the common ward. Before then, upon entering the kitchen, she comes face to face

---

* Paulina Salas is the chief protagonist of *Death and the Maiden* (1990) by the Chilean playwright Ariel Dorfman. A former political prisoner, Paulina has survived rape by her captors, including a doctor whose face she never saw but whose voice and mannerisms she recognises later when her husband, Gerardo Escobar, brings him to their home. The play was adapted for the screen in 1994.

again with Paulina Salas, who invites her to join her the following day for coffee. The young woman accepts and promises to bring cream puffs. Paulina seems thrilled, and says she'll teach her pastry-making if she likes. The woman prays to God her opening gambit won't disgrace her.

The next day, Paulina Salas is waiting for her in Room 3. The young woman enters with a tray of cream puffs. Paulina becomes very excited. She shakes and shakes her curly head and pours the coffee.

'You're very beautiful, Paulina.'

'Right back at you, Young Woman.'

Paulina hums the theme of *Death and the Maiden*. She takes a slow, sumptuous bite of her cream puff and pronounces it superb. They get to talking. But then a voice rings out that makes Paulina's face fall. She knows that voice, she explains.

Paulina was arrested in wintertime. The interrogations, pressure and brutality ran through to spring, then summer. One day at the height of it all, the man whose voice they had heard gave her back her clothes – her own clothes, not prison garments – and told her: 'Get ready. We're going to meet your family.' Paulina, dressed in winter clothes, emerged blinking into the sun. Flanked by the man with the voice and a group of others, she was taken to a parking lot outside a multi-storey apartment block. They told her to go to the third floor, where someone would be waiting for her.

Paulina was scared. She knew perfectly well that visitation facilities wouldn't be there, in a suburban tower block. What could she do? She resisted; they insisted. She cried and begged them to take her back to her cell, and in the end, they gave up and put her back in the car. But they drove her to a shopping centre. Surrounded by plainclothes officers, she was in no position to shout, as she wanted to: *'Help! I'm Paulina Salas and they've kidnapped me!'*

The man with the voice told her to go into one of the shops and pick out some clothes for him. Paulina burst into tears there, in the middle of the thoroughfare. 'I'm not your wife,' she said. The man with the voice didn't understand; in his eyes, every woman was his wife. She demanded again to be taken back to her cell, but he took her to a restaurant instead.

It was a dreadful restaurant, with nobody there but plainclothes officers. The man with the voice and his colleagues ordered an array of entrées, desserts and beverages, and ate and drank their fill, laughing uproariously all the while. Paulina wondered what would happen to her, and why they wouldn't take her back.

They put Paulina in the car again and took her to a sprawling, lavishly furnished villa. Naked men in the pool mocked Paulina for crying so much, and made sex jokes at her expense. They might have been officers, too; she wasn't sure. Frightened, Paulina tried to take refuge in a toilet, and when she opened the doors to the bedroom she saw the hidden cameras.

By sunset, Paulina knew the laughter of the naked men in the pool by heart. Each and every one of them.

When she hears the voice, she gets up, leaves Room 3, and attends to it. Then she comes back, by which time her coffee has gone cold and the young woman has gone back to her bunk.

The young woman finally opens the book. As she does so, a letter falls out from between the pages. It's dated more than ten years earlier, and simply signed: *N. D.*

It's Saturday night on the 6th of January. We are seven restless people.

'Are the props for Scene 1 in place?'

'Where's the blue mica sheet?'

'The middle table's not fully straight.'

'Nothing we can do about it now. They're all in their seats.'

'Should we get started? Shall we turn off the lights?'

'Do it.'

Darkness. After a few seconds, a blue light illuminates the stage. It's a bedroom scene. The door to the ward storeroom opens. Enter Player One.

'Hello! I'm Paulina Salas!'

It was about a week ago that we, the seven good players of the Evin Theatre Company, staged our adaptation of Ariel Dorfman's *Death and the Maiden* in the downstairs gym. Theatre has always fascinated me. It has a magic I can't describe, which I've felt at almost every rehearsal I've been involved in, let alone performances. But my experience of it here behind bars, of the process of writing and rehearsing every day for the sake of a single night, has been something else. I hadn't understood the essence of theatre before now.

They say it isn't right to review one's own creation, but I'm going to say it: we did a spectacular job, even though not one of the women had a background in theatre, and might not even have known anything about it before now. I devoured every hour we spent practising, and greedily recorded every moment in my mind. We received no material support or equipment, save for a single classical music CD brought in from outside. They poured all their effort into the props, the lighting, scenery, the music and the acting.

Paulina Salas, armed with a cardboard gun and a CD player, mesmerised the audience. Gerardo Escobar, her husband, stood on the terrace of the villa (which we'd made by tying together metal bookshelves from the library). Under the light of the reading lamps our operators had turned blue by sticking blue mica sheets over them, he articulated his helplessness and devastation. Not merely Paulina, but the whole audience, was convinced and willing to forgive him.

We dedicated our single performance to Iran's Paulinas. Perhaps some of them were there in the audience.

PAULINA SALAS

Theatre is the art of life, and life runs through it. For me, staging a play in prison, which most of us believe is a period of dormancy and stagnation, is a manifestation of hope. Our play expressed voices that have yet to be silenced, and aspirations that have not yet closed their wings. All this, in a place which by its very design exists only to oppose these things.

We missed you all on Saturday. At the same time, though, we felt your presence. It's why I asked the esteemed head of the prison in writing to let us perform for the other inmates as well.

More than anything else, I hope that, not so long from now, the wonderful day will come when the Evin Theatre Company stands before you in a real theatre, and Paulina can greet you in person.*

Nazanin dedicated the play to all the Paulinas of Iran, whose existence is so much plainer to us now.

---

* *Death and the Maiden* was performed on 5 January 2013, on the women's ward of Evin Prison. The director (and the author of this letter) was Nazanin Deyhimi, a translator, actress and women's rights activist who was jailed for 'propaganda against the regime'. She died from an asthma attack in 2017. The cast comprised Deyhimi, Shiva Nazar Ahari, Mahsa Amrabadi, Nasim Soltan Baigi and Bahareh Hedayat.

The Paulinas of Iran know by heart the sounds of the laughter of men who leave bruises on their bodies in the corners of cells. They know the smell of them, even the pace of their footsteps. One day the Paulinas will hunt down the possessors of those voices, although they won't be able to entrust them to the courts when they do. Until then, the sound of any door opening at midnight will remind them of what was done to them. Resistance isn't their only weapon. They can also keep reminding the voices: *we shall not forget.* In so doing, they keep the Roberto Mirandas – the torturers – of Iran afraid, forever.

We, in turn, present cream puffs to all the Paulinas. We honour and express our gratitude to each of the Paulinas in that gym twelve years ago, and to Nazanin Deyhimi, who, with her art, struck a blow to the prison's steel carapace that still reverberates down the hallways today. Hail her untainted soul, an embodiment of hope.

EIGHT
Saving Tuesdays

It's Tuesday. For the young woman, all Tuesdays are cursed with monotony. In primary school it was the day they taught maths, science and dictation, and somehow at secondary school all the most stultifying classes were crammed into Tuesdays, too. The Evin Prison weekly schedule is irrefutable proof, to her, that Tuesdays are a lost cause. Inmates can't even use the phone on Tuesdays – only Mondays, Wednesdays, Fridays and Saturdays – and the anxiety of no news is as malignant as cancer. It makes her wonder if news has gotten out, if she's been disgraced outside yet. On Tuesdays she feels cold and fidgety. Just like the science lessons, it feels like there's no end in sight.

There is a silver lining, though. The young woman has befriended an inmate who's spent every Tuesday for the last thirteen years dancing, laughing, exercising and reading, with only minor variations from one week to the next. In the bleakest weekday night, this woman brings the comforting aroma of caraway. Up at dawn, she seems to fill the whole day with activities. Then, as the day draws to a close, she invites all the young women on the ward – cold, bored, disgraced, not yet disgraced – to come and join her at seven o'clock for a bowl of *adasi* with caraway.* They can talk, laugh, posture, ask questions about the recipe, or just sit quietly and listen to her reminisce.

The young woman hasn't had the energy to look after herself lately. She's lost a lot of blood. Judging by her sunken eyes, she suspects the Tuesday woman is anaemic too. Nevertheless, this one finds the motivation to take care of not just herself but the other women on the ward. She has no interest in the young woman's condition; she just doles out the *adasi*, and that's it.

Gradually, because of evenings like these, Tuesdays take on a warmer hue. The *adasi* feasts make the young

---

* *Adasi* is a type of Iranian pottage with lentils as the primary ingredient, seasoned with onions, dried mint and spices (often turmeric). It can also feature tomato paste, mincemeat and/or potato.

woman laugh more. She regains some of her strength. She listens, charmed, to the other women's stories, and is so taken by them she'll spend all of Wednesday reviewing them in her head. The things that frightened her before are lost to a haze of caraway and memories. If she's disgraced now, cut off from the world, perhaps it won't matter after all. The caraway has done its job. Finally, the young woman looks forward to Tuesdays.

'I'll start making pastries to serve with *adasi* and caraway,' she volunteers. The woman, whom she's called Goli (meaning rosy), likes the sound of that very much.

Every apple in the world has a touch of Goli in it. Without the colour and scent of apples, this world wouldn't be what it is. It's not the name this woman was born with. But when she laughs, both her cheeks are like a round, rosy red apple, whole and complete, and it makes life worth living. Her laughter is a masterpiece. Goli has been laughing at tyrants, and everything else besides, for thirteen years now. Her laughter is as red as can be, and as bracing. When she laughs, we all stand taller. Her laughter is rebellion. All these years, nobody has ever seen her cry.

It's in honour of those perfect apple cheeks that the young woman starts baking apple pies and apple tarts on Tuesdays, alternating each week. Now Tuesdays also have the aroma of cinnamon. 'Smells incredible!' the inmates yell on arrival, and the young woman explains that it's the smell of Goli's laughter. But Goli's real name is Maryam Akbari Monfared.

Maryam is community. She binds together all the women who've rebelled, transgressed, or both. Mothers seeking justice, sisters seeking justice: as one, they pass along and retain a smile that never fully disappears. Maryam is faithful to the community, and keeps their collective work alive – collective work, collective merriment, collective dancing, collective grief, collective justice-seeking, collective slogan-chanting, collective protest, collective compromise. But in so doing, Maryam also stays faithful to her own nature. Not once, not even on Nowruz, the winter solstice, or the anniversary of the November 2019 protests does she fail to gather them together in the hall to sing at the top of their voices, right in front of the CCTV cameras. Prison or the street, it makes no difference: wherever she is, Maryam will draw hands together to form a circle of sisters, and they'll sing the revolutionary anthem 'Blood of the Redbuds' (*Khune Arghavanha*).* This is the legacy of the caraway Tuesdays, a masterclass in solidarity.

There are ten very simple pastries named after Maryam, which you can bake for anybody who's been separated from their community. Ideally, you should bake them on the eve of Nowruz. Find one another, hold each other's hands and sing the song. Address it to those whose hands have been separated from yours. Maryam likes to have these pastries on celebrations, or on any occasion where women have gathered.

---

* 'Blood of the Redbuds' was composed by Saeed Soltanpour and released by the Organisation of Iranian People's Fedai Guerrillas on a cassette tape 'Sparks of the Sun' (*Sharareha-ye Aftab*) in 1979.

Recipe 12

Apple pie
for Maryam Akbari Monfared

◆ ◆ ◆

Just like Maryam herself, this apple pie has unrivalled taste. It's tender, and comes apart in your mouth with the aroma of apples and cinnamon. We'll have to make several. Cornflour is the key to success here, so be sure to include it.

INGREDIENTS

350g flour	1 tbsp baking powder
5 eggs	4 tbsp cornflour
2 tbsp icing sugar	3 apples
250g sugar	3 tbsp chopped walnuts
250g softened butter	cinnamon, to taste
¼ tsp vanilla	

DIRECTIONS

Keep the butter at near-melting temperature for an hour or so before you start. Put on the song 'Your Memento' (*Sanin Yadegarin*) by Rastak Ensemble. If you've got long hair, let it down. Bob your head in time with the music while baking.

Beat the eggs and add them to the softened butter. That is, add one egg, lip-sync or mumble to the Azerbaijani song, toss your hair, and add the next one, and then the next in exactly the same way. Gradually mix in the flour, sugar, cornflour and baking powder. Core and cut the apples into rings, restart the song, and coat the apples in the cinnamon, vanilla and icing sugar in a separate bowl.

Use about half of the dough mix to line the base of a pie tin. You can use a piping bag if it's easier. Arrange the apple slices and chopped walnuts over the top of it, then pour another layer of the dough mix over the top. Bake the tart in the oven at 180°C for 20–30 minutes. Towards the end, you can sprinkle a little more icing sugar over the top.

Now remove your aromatic apple pie from the oven and dance a while longer. If you have a companion, whirl around together and then tuck in with a cup of tea. If you don't know any dances, watch a couple of videos online. There's no need to be a professional. Toss your head, rejoice.

◆ ◆ ◆

MARYAM DANCES, tosses her hair about. As summer turns into autumn, she dances a Turkish dance and laughs a Turkish laugh in the same space where countless others have come and gone over thirteen years. They are gone, but she has stayed. Her dance is impassioned, joyous. She dismisses the night with her feet. The brightest part of our darkened world is Maryam, who imbues new life into our bruised hearts with each fresh rotation. For these thirteen years, she's been neither undone by repetition nor tired out by twirling. It's not just she who will survive this way; she makes others want to follow her, too.

Maryam Akbari Monfared was born in December 1975. In 2009, she was taken away from her three-year-old daughter, from the small beauty shop she owned, and from their modest home, and came to Evin Prison. She brought her search for justice, her rosy colour palette and her boundless love to this place. As anyone who's met her will testify, she doesn't know how to capitulate or obey, only how to stand tirelessly in the face of tyranny in any shape or form. Anyone who's spent a year, an hour, or even a moment at Evin will recall something of her, and it'll be a memory that stirs that person, makes her whisper to herself: '*I wish I were Maryam, too.*' Or even more boldly: '*I am Maryam Akbari Monfared.*'

Maryam's is a luminous chapter in the history of Iranian women. It won't be erased no matter how hard anyone tries; her every cry of excitement and jubilation is etched on too many hearts. One day, the heirs to generations of injustice will line up with bouquets of red roses just for her, all the way from Evin to Khavaran.*

Shortly after Ebrahim Raisi was appointed head of the Iranian judiciary in 2019, there was a flurry of activity at Evin. Officials scrambled to make Tehran's flagship penitentiary look passable. They changed the water pipes, replaced the light fittings and polished the cage bars. This incensed Maryam. She wasn't having any of it. She got up from her bunk and bellowed: 'Raisi will not wash away the blood that's been shed by installing new taps! I am a claimant, and my case is against him!'

---

* Khavaran Cemetery in southeastern Tehran is the site of a mass grave. In 1988, at the close of the Iran–Iraq war, thousands of political detainees were slaughtered in prisons up and down the country in a matter of weeks, systematically and on the orders of then-Supreme Leader Ayatollah Khomeini. Most of the victims' bodies were never identified or turned over to their families.

And so it came to pass that in the middle of her eleventh year in prison, Maryam filed a formal complaint against Ebrahim Raisi with an international court.*

We learned something from her that day. We learned that we could all take on the role of plaintiff in the case against those who'd gladly act as the arbiters of criminal behaviour. It was possible to cry out from behind bars and to have the sound travel beyond the walls.

---

* Ebrahim Raisi, who became President of Iran in June 2021, was complicit in Iran's 1988 prison massacre. That summer, as a then-junior prosecutor, he sat on a four-member 'death panel' in Tehran that decided the fates of prisoners based on the answer each gave to a single yes/no question. In February 2017, Maryam Akbari Monfared filed a complaint with the UN Working Group on Forced or Involuntary Disappearances, demanding justice for her own four siblings and the thousands of others who were shot or hanged that summer.

NINE
Sharing Dreams with Fatu

THIS ONE IS A WANDERER, somewhere on the boundary line between reality and fantasy. Her name is Fatemeh, or 'Fatu' in the Bushehri dialect. Generally, when she talks about who she was or what happened to her, she stumbles into the fantastical side. But the illusions are so detailed, so intricately plotted and minutely described, they might as well be real. Soon enough, the listener trips over the border with her. A woman of the world is our Fatu.

Regardless of whether they're true, you'll come to notice that Fatu's stories contain the same three protagonists: her uncle, her brother and her Kuwaiti aunt. All three have died in the time she's been here – that part's real. Five years, she's served so far in Bushehr Prison – that part, too, is definitely real. Fatu hails from the city of Borazjan in Bushehr Province, and it seems likely that she's serving time for debt.

Fatu's like a child, and when she wants something, she's got to have it *all*, immediately. She often gets into scrapes with the other inmates, and then gets beaten and cursed out, because she hogs the phone long past the allotted 10 minutes. Not that there's much love for her at the other end of the line, either. All her phone conversations seem to revolve around money. The longer she yammers on, the more likely she seems to believe that something will drop into her account. When it does, Fatu orders Turkish kebabs or fish sandwiches for every inmate on the ward – even the women who beat her up and cursed her in the line for the phone, and the women who looked on, unmoved, as it happened. When Fatu's pocket is full, everybody's is full. Indeed, one of the cases against her is over a 25 million-*toman* ($430) debt she racked up by repeatedly buying fruit for the ward.

In total, Fatu has served eight years. Being overly generous with everything that comes her way is probably what put her here. Her Kuwaiti aunt is famous in Bushehr Prison, and a hugely important part of the Fatu mythos: six years ago, this Kuwaiti aunt bought every single fridge and water cooler going for the inmates

SHARING DREAMS WITH FATU

on the ward. Many of them grew up at her table, so to speak. But there was a catch – isn't there always – and now Fatu owes a pile of money to the home-appliances company. Her pronouncements on her Kuwaiti aunt are the stuff of legend. They've been quoted and requoted so many times, they've taken on the quality of an oral history. It's still not completely clear that the aunt exists; nevertheless, we pray nightly for her.

Before the emergence of this aunt, Fatu had, at one stage, a Lebanese aunt, apparently since retired. 'Once I was in Lebanon to visit my aunt,' she'd declaim, 'and after a week, my aunt told me: "Now you've come all this way, do pay a visit to Egypt as well."' Fatu, the story goes, got on a jet ski and struck out from Lebanese waters for Egypt. But the Israelis spotted her, shot at the craft and forcibly returned her to Iran. The first time Fatu told this story, we fell about laughing – and that was just at the suggestion of an Egyptian holiday. But so emphatic and detailed was her description of the Israelis' faces and uniforms, we couldn't help but respect it.

In her own telling, Fatu's a wheeler-dealer. She's got connections in all the military and judicial bodies worth knowing about, and for 10 million *tomans* ($170) she can get your case wiped clean off the slate. Heck, even a murder charge – they can make it go away. Fatu's especially fond of political prisoners, though, because her uncle was a big hitter in the Supreme Leader's office, and it just so happens that if you bung 5 million *tomans* ($85) into her account (that's the discounted rate), he can send the worst national-security case Iran's ever seen up in flames as if it never happened. Of course, in the unlikely event your case stays on the books, Fatu's having bought 5 million *tomans*' worth of pizza and drinks for the ward that same afternoon will be a total coincidence. The Kuwaiti aunt paid for it.

The young woman first encounters Fatu while the latter is kissing the prison warden's feet and begging his forgiveness. It's a jarring scene. The previous night, she'd heard Fatu talking in whispers with another inmate after dark, which is completely not allowed in Bushehr. Now here she is, kissing the warden's feet. How does this happen?

The young woman recalls what she knows about Fatu's past punishments:

1. Fatu is deeply religious. She gets up at five o'clock in the morning to pray. Before she does, she goes to the bathroom to make her ablutions, and has to use a bottle of mineral water because the tap water's been cut off. Someone alerts the prison warden. They take her out into the yard, strip her and make her wash herself with milk.
2. Fatu is hygiene-obsessed. Well, she's not, actually; the steps she takes are the same ones any free woman would take to keep clean and healthy. But her behaviour still provokes the ire of the warden, who doesn't regard inmates as human beings. As punishment, she is not allowed to wear slippers for a month. The ground is so hot, she even tries wearing freezer bags around her feet to ease the pain. It doesn't work. 'The burns and humiliation make me cry every night,' she tells a fellow inmate. 'I've cried harder than I did for my brother.'
3. Fatu is told that if she wants to be granted leave, she's got to buy things such as fridges and television sets 'for the prison'. Somehow she manages to do so. Fatu also yields to demands for bribes

in order to make the abuse stop. This lands her in deeper debt – and of course, it never stops.

4. Fatu calls her friend noisily from the prison's 'cultural hub', a sacred zone in which talking in raised voices is a grave offence. They punish her by making her stand on one foot in the 60°C heat, and force all her cellmates to boo her. (Here the young woman falls silent, then says: 'As I've said before, Bushehr Prison and its abuses differ from the rest. The military-style discipline there is the stuff of movies, like in *The Shawshank Redemption*.')

5. Fatu is kicked so hard in the side that her kidney haemorrhages.

6. Fatu is undressed in front of everyone, and her underwear is taken away from her. They do this so she'll scream about the lack of hygiene the next time she has her period.

7. Fatu is quarantined for weeks.

8. Fatu is beaten.

9. Fatu has a new case opened against her.

10. Fatu is beaten.

11. Fatu is beaten.

12. Fatu is undressed.

13. Fatu is undressed.
14. Fatu is forced to apologise for something in the most degrading way.
15. Fatu is beaten.
16. Fatu is beaten again.

In prison, what counts as a sin is different. Fatu is being tortured to an extent she's never experienced before in her life because she talked loudly, or kept leftovers from lunch for dinner. There are a lot of Fatus here, but nobody's much of a friend to anybody else, because friendship leads to empathy – and that is absolutely forbidden. Even talking *sotto voce* with a guard is, technically, an offence. Inmates have to wear a *chador* and *hijab* at all times in Bushehr, and removing either is an offence, except while sleeping. Being a human being is forbidden. Dancing, obviously, is forbidden.

The young woman tries, gently, to get close to Fatu. She talks to her about tasty pastries, and Fatu's eyes shine. The battering she's taken makes her afraid of friendship. But in the end, gluttony gets the better of her. The young woman uses her own connections to set up a kitchen. Fatu bends over backwards to get placed there as the sales manager.

'You look like my Kuwaiti aunt's housemaid,' she tells the young woman, who looks alarmed. 'Because you are so smart,' she adds quickly.

Their alliance doesn't go unnoticed. As a result, Fatu is beaten again, and cut off from using the phone. The young woman tries to defend her, but her interventions only make it worse. Fatu doesn't crumble. 'Not important,' she says. 'I've had enough of getting trashed and blinded in prison.' (*Trashed and blinded* is a Bushehri expression that, it's since been explained to me, connotes being warped or deformed by the environment. It's said that any woman – lover, mother, beautiful pink-cheeked local girl – can bed down for the night in prison and wake up the following morning horribly transmuted into a professional detainee, as though she's been in Bushehr Prison for one hundred years.)

But one day, while Fatu's crying again over the punishments meted out to her, the young woman decides that, as she can't really do anything for her, she ought to distance herself from Fatu. Fatu approaches her, and she steps back. Fatu begins to cry again.

SHARING DREAMS WITH FATU

Sometime later, she writes the young woman a letter. It begins with a poem:

Hopeful I am for a kindness from my friend,
A great wrong have I done, and her forgiveness I dream of.
Certain I am that she will forgive the wrong that I have done,
For a fairy she might be, but a true angel she is.*

Now it's the young woman's turn to cry. In desperation, she goes to the pastry kitchen to make Fatu's favourite, *logaimat*, a kind of Arab dumpling.

---

* These lines are by Hafez, one of the greatest and most beloved Persian classical poets.

Recipe 13

*Logaimat
for Fatu*

◆ ◆ ◆

INGREDIENTS

480g flour
1 egg
240ml cooking oil
240ml date syrup

1 tsp baker's yeast
2 tbsp cornflour
1 cup water

DIRECTIONS

Add the yeast to the flour and slowly pour in the water, mixing as you go. Place in a covered container and leave somewhere warm for a couple of hours, until the dough has risen. Mix the beaten egg and cornflour together, then combine with the dough. Heat the oil and use a funnel to drop the mixture in little blobs or small squares into the frying pan. Once the *logaimat* are fried, remove them with a spatula and coat them in the date syrup. Roll in desiccated coconut if you feel fancy.

◆ ◆ ◆

SHARING DREAMS WITH FATU

THE NEXT DAY Fatu is beaten again, and the kitchen is shut down permanently. The woman considers Fatu: her favourite pastry, her getting trashed and blinded, her fables, the abuses she suffers, her visit to Lebanon, her Kuwaiti aunt. She wishes she hadn't gotten close to Fatu. All she did was become a new catalyst for more torture.

Without knowing it, Fatu had been the one in a position to help. One of the things they'd discussed at length and in great detail was a friend of the young woman's with silvery hair, whose absence she still wept over. The friend's name was Sepideh Kashani.

Fatu had probed further, asking the young woman to tell her more. Fatu had been a fisherwoman just like Kashi. Perhaps they'd met before, somewhere at sea.

TEN

The National Library of Nostalgia

KASHI, the young woman tries to explain, is a bundle of nostalgic feelings. Nostalgia comes in different forms, and in Kashi they are all gathered together in a single human vessel. Most people try to rid themselves of the urge to reminisce, especially when it brings pain. But Kashi retains and curates every second, every segment, every facet of and every link to nostalgia, and arranges them in the display cabinets within her, with a special perfectionist discipline: a sort of national library of nostalgia.

There's a specific writer and style for each object of nostalgia. For Houman Jokar, it's Romain Gary. For Sima, the young woman's sister, it's Louis-Ferdinand Céline. For her schoolfriend, it's Milan Kundera. It's worth noting here that each nostalgic episode has no bearing whatsoever on the impact of the next. Each has its own, independently associated pain, and, just as critically, its own weight. The build-up of too many nostalgias in the chest can cause an avalanche that slides down the body, lower and lower. That's what happened to Kashi. Her weight fell off her chest and piled up below the waist.

Her hair is silvery. Tears rush frantically from her tear ducts, join one another in brief, spectacular unity, then fall unceremoniously. Her eyes are even more gorgeous when she cries. You can't take your own eyes off them.

More than this, Kashi is a colossal support. You can lean on the curves of her body and not fall down. The nostalgia that shapes her makes her a saviour. If someone's upset, it's impossible for her to be indifferent. She's a mother without claiming or wanting to be one. Just as well, because she's also a child: your playmate when you're splashing around in the water in summertime, an eighty-year-old when the time comes to mourn a loved one. Always in love, always nostalgic, always laser-focused in empathy and in sympathy, that's Kashi.

Her existence means confidence. Confidence that, out of this maelstrom—

Fatu interrupts. 'Kashani's got to be one of two myths, yes? First possibility, she's a mermaid and that's why she's got this curved lower body. Probably it glows, as well. If you see her, it means wealth and an end to your run of bad luck, and any fisherman who comes across her makes a killing.' She warms to her theme: 'As a fisherwoman, I believe we have come to know the mermaids better through Kashi than to know Kashi through mermaids.'

The young woman is taken aback.

'The second possibility is the moving island.' Fatu won't say more. 'The Gulf is just around the corner, so I'll leave that one to you. Go to the sea and figure it out for yourself.'

Previously, the young woman had believed Kashi was an elephant, like those in Romain Gary's novel *The Roots of Heaven*: firm, unshakeable structures that people can cling to during high tides of loneliness and alienation. Houman's love for her is exactly of this kind. Houman is Morrel, the novel's protagonist, for whom the elephant is an emblem of Nature. Kashi is both Nature and elephant.

When elephants lose a loved one, they mourn for so long over its body that eventually they die in the same spot. The young woman remembers Kashi during the

mourning rites they held for Kavous Seyed-Emami.*
While making *halva* and tearing out her hair, she'd
had the air of a tribal woman who'd committed her
child's body to the mountains, just as Kavous had been.
Mourning seemed to make her grow taller. In the interrogation room they'd shown her a picture of Kavous's body
and a video of the lamentations of Maryam, Kavous's wife.

Deadpan, she'd asked: 'You killed him?'

But Fatu's Kashi-as-mermaid hypothesis is also compelling. One doesn't have to look hard to find traces of
the mermaid in Iranian mythology and scholarship on
the wonders of the world. One of the fantastic stories
in Shahriyar al-Ramhormuzi's *The Book of the Wonders
of India* describes a group of Iranian seafarers who find
themselves in a gulf inhabited by humanoid sea creatures
with silky skin. So light and nimble are they, it's easy to
imagine them taking to the skies at a moment's notice.
They have small heads and underwater breathing apparatus on their backs below the shoulders, like sea turtles.

---

* Kavous Seyed-Emami, an environmentalist and the founder of the Persian Wildlife Heritage Foundation, was one of the eight conservationists arrested in January 2018. He died under suspicious circumstances in Evin Prison two days later, in what the Iranian judiciary claimed was suicide.

In *The Wonders of Creation and the Oddities of Existence*, Zakaria Qazvini describes marine entities that look just like human beings, save for the lower parts of their bodies. The story goes that a merman is brought to the surface and offered as a gift to a king. But no one can understand what he's trying to say. The king procures a wife for him, and when their child is born, it's raised bilingually to get around the problem. An illustration in the book depicts a fish with a human torso and head.

In *The Book of Darab* by Tarsusi, a mermaid falls in love with a human. They marry in the end. And in *The Book of Alexander*, the poet Nezami speaks of mermaids who come to the shore at night and lure mariners off-course. Mermaids have emerged from the waves in contemporary Persian poetry as well, as in Nima Yooshij's *Maneli*, which depicts a fisherman spellbound by a woman from the deep.

Little by little, the young woman becomes convinced that Kashi is, indeed, a mermaid. She recalls that, one night after Goli finished dancing, Kashi stood up and continued the cycle of the dance into infinity. May mermaids surface each and every night from that estuary, as regularly as the sun and moon rise! Their dancing is a keepsake, and it's been entrusted to the right person – a mermaid. The young woman thinks of Fayez, the folk poet from Bushehr's Dashti region, who also fell in love with one of them. He ended up confessing to his wife, and she left him. Now alone, in his mind he leaves for the sea. He hums a poem: '*O Fairy! Old I might be but not sorrowful, for my love is young. O Fairy! This young love is all still to come.*'

FOURTH LETTER

Greetings, my dearest! Greetings, my only dearest. The people of the south have a fable about something called 'the moving island'. In the story, a fisherman gets caught in a storm and is swallowed up by the sea. When he comes around, he finds himself on a big, safe spit of land. But it's no ordinary island. It moves all the time. One morning, he wakes to see he's close to the coast where his hometown is. The island moves closer and closer, and he's able to jump for it. When he does, he realises he'd sat all this time on the backside of a gigantic creature.

Houman's love. Sima. Amirsalar. The older girl called Kashi. Dear Shahla, and so many others: they all found refuge on your moving island when life's problems threatened to drown them. What I want to say is that your big ass has been the saviour of us all, to say nothing of your eyes and hands and heart. The letter I'm writing to you now is going to be censored by several people, from soldiers to agents of the State. But I learned from you that love cannot be censored or made to end.

The young woman is confused. Is Kashi an elephant, a mermaid, or a moving island? It seems to have varied, depending on the time of day. She remembers when three of their fellow inmates – Yasaman Aryani, Monireh Arabshahi and Samaneh Nowruz-Moradi – were suddenly removed from the ward all at once.*

---

* Monireh Arabshahi and Yasaman Aryani, mother and daughter, were imprisoned in April 2019 after their peaceful protest against mandatory hijab on International Women's Day's went viral. They were released in February 2023. Samaneh Nowruz-Moradi was arrested for membership of opposition groups in 2018. She was sent to serve her sentence in Evin Prison in 2019. She was released in 2021, but was rearrested in 2023, and remains in Evin Prison.

They'd only gone to meet their lawyer, but they never returned. Joy left the ward in their wake. Everyone was bewildered by what seemed, on the face of it, to have been an abduction. The state of their bunks suggested they hadn't expected to be gone long.

Kashi alone put the broken pieces of the ward back together. She'd never claimed to be a skilled orator, but delivered a speech that was, in every way, pitch-perfect: 'If this ward is a human body,' she began, 'today we lost three of the organs.' And she was right. At breakfast, she brought new life to us all, pulled us back into the circle of the dance and insisted we not cave in. In the course of that day she was the elephant we leaned on, the mermaid that brought us prosperity, joy and song, the island that saved us from drowning.

Every Wednesday, Kashi goes to visit a man who has dedicated his whole life to the natural world. She bakes cookies to take with her to Houman, and sometimes the young woman has the privilege of helping her. Houman loves peanut butter. He can't stand pastries that are too sweet, and he prefers them simple and small. So, under Sepideh Kashani's guidance, the young woman bakes cookies for Houman.

Recipe 14

Peanut butter cookies
for Houman Jokar and Sepideh Kashani

◆ ◆ ◆

INGREDIENTS

250g flour
1–2 tbsp peanut butter (depending on your taste, which has nothing to do with us)
70g icing sugar
the tip of a teaspoonful of vanilla
70g butter
walnuts, chopped, to taste
2 eggs

DIRECTIONS

First, put on the song 'Always a Helping Hand' (*Yavareh Hamisheh Momen*) by Dariush Eghbali. Houman is always a helping hand. Our Sepideh hums the song, too.

Separate the egg whites from the yolks, keeping both. Chop the walnuts into small pieces (don't crush them). Cream the butter, icing sugar and vanilla, then add the egg yolks and mix. Add the flour in stages. Finally, stir in the peanut butter. Knead with your own two faithful helping hands until the mixture no longer sticks to them. Then take small amounts of the dough at a time, roll into balls, dip into the leftover egg whites and roll in the chopped walnuts. Lay out on a lined oven tray and bake for 15 minutes at 180°C, until golden. When they're ready, separate them carefully from the greaseproof paper. I can lean on you, dear cookie.

◆ ◆ ◆

ELEVEN

In Praise of Marzieh Amiri

'They asked me if I wanted Marzieh.' I said: 'I want her like the East and West want Syria.'*

It's five o'clock in the morning in Bushehr. All the inmates receive from the Persian Gulf over here is a wicked wind. They've got to get up at five in the morning and stand in the full blast of it, swathed in *chadors*, no less, for morning calisthenics. Nobody has the right to refuse. *One ... two ... three ... four ... five ... six ...*

This morning they stripped a new arrival in the roll-call line. She had refused to take part in the exercises the day before. The exercise session is just the start of the catalogue daily humiliations, all of which take place while wearing *chadors*. Those who deviate even

---

* Marzieh Amiri is a journalist for the reformist *Shargh* newspaper. She was one of more than fifty reporters who were arrested between September and December 2022 amid pro-democracy protests in Iran.

in minor ways will pay dearly. After being forced to read the *Surah an-Nur*, you might be beaten, lose your visitation rights or phone calls, or have a new criminal case opened against you. Or they might strip you down in the yard to make your ablutions.

It's now seven o'clock in the evening. The new arrival, Kobra Behyari, has committed murder. For a full twenty-four hours before it happened, she'd been tortured by her husband. At exactly five o'clock in the morning he'd taken away her phone, locked every door in the house, forced her into an 'interrogation' chair and demanded she confess to having been with another man. The woman refused, stunned, and he tortured her for a full day. Still, she didn't confess. 'That night I pissed myself a few times,' she said. 'But I kept telling myself it would be better for me to be the only one who dies, not anybody else.' At a quarter to five the following morning, the man told her she had five minutes left: 'If you don't confess, you'll be dead.' He was on the verge of pulling the trigger when she grabbed the gun. In the struggle, the gun discharged. The bullet hit a light fitting, ricocheted, hit the man and killed him.

Now in her seventh year of incarceration, Kobra has been assigned to the staff canteen. Every morning she sweeps the floor and feeds the staff, hoping that one of these days they'll bring her news of forgiveness from her husband's relatives. Lately, she's been shouting a lot: 'For God's sake, just execute me! I can't take it any more!'

The prosecutor's representative comes to see her. He wants her to confirm exactly what she was doing with that other man. It's not a name he wants, or the circumstances. He wants the details of their affair. 'Tell me about his dick size,' he entreats her. 'Did it go in easily or not? How many times a day did he fuck you?'

She leaves the office dazed, and crashes immediately on her bunk.

Another day, in another time, a woman with a fringe is returning from work. As she walks, she hums 'The Judge Loved Me' (*Ghazi Mano Doosht Dasht*) a song by Soroush Hichkas.

Today, Kobra's shoulders ache badly. She can't get her underwear on and takes off her bra, hoping to hide the absence of both under a baggy dress. *No one will notice,* she thinks. But the female warden gets wind of it and summons the woman before her and the supervising judge.

It starts with a barrage of insults. The inmate tries to explain she's done nothing illegal, and in any event there shouldn't be anybody on the ward but other women. The warden – who herself habitually wears a skirt, nail polish and see-through tights – turns to the supervising judge. 'These women are a bunch of horny deviants. Her not wearing a bra is a signal to the other lesbians.'

The inmate is thunderstruck. *How is this happening?* She can't speak, and turns bright red. The judge, whom she had earlier thought of as being of sound mind, just smiles at her and asks the warden to leave. The warden does so. 'Well,' says the judge. The woman barrels out the door.

Some distance away, a woman with a fringe is leaving home in the cool of springtime. She glances at the horizon. Somewhere out there, a thousand kilometres from where she stands, is a place where dumbstruck women barrel out of doors. '*The judge loved me*', she hums.

Inside Bushehr, they're saying there's going to be an inspection. The women are in the kitchen, baking. They're hoping against hope that their last refuge in a place already proximate to Hell won't be shut down. A man enters: the big boss. They take the inmate back to the office. A little while later, she returns in a daze.

They want her to give a taped confession. The prospect is unthinkable, as is the converse: she'll be finished if she talks, and finished if she doesn't. Her friends plead with her, and she listens to them. She goes back and says the words into the camera that the prison officials want her to say. The camera is turned off. The inmate exits the room, rubs her face. Then she shouts: 'People, I have been violated!'

A woman named Marzieh comes out of the alley. She's still humming 'The Judge Loved Me', on and on. At the end of the alley where Marzieh has been walking stands a prison for violated women. Standing before it now, she represents them all. She shakes out her fringe and, as loudly as she can, recites the verses she's written for her friends inside.

You'd never guess by looking at her that her voice is as strong as it is. She shakes out her fringe, and it's as if she's been present in every room in which a judge has ever 'loved' a female detainee, and she defies their violation now. It's as if it's Marzieh herself, who was violated in the corner of that room. Now she dares them to hold hands and shout: 'We have been violated!'

At the end of the poem, she smiles and says: 'Feminism taught me this.'

This moment will stand as an emblem of empathy for and between the women who have been violated. Together, with faces burned by acid and bodies bruised by the lashes of belts, they'll swarm out and over the wall to run, hold one another's hands and sing: *'Feminism taught me this.'* A woman with a fringe rapping in the streets of Tehran has given them a lesson in feminism.

Recipe 15

Madeleines for Marzieh Amiri

◆ ◆ ◆

These are a taste of Marzieh. They're pretty, but they don't need cream or other decorations to be so. Simple, but with good taste. Carries a heavy load, but doesn't complain. I'm talking about Marzieh here.

To make madeleines, you need madeleine moulds, which you can buy from a homeware shop. They look like oysters. Pretty, no? Put on 'The Kerb and the Dream' (*Jadval o Roya*) by the rapper Soroush Hichkas. Marzieh loves rap. Just like the lyrics, this baking is fast. It's easy and lasts a long time, and it's risk-free, like a friendship with Marzieh. It fits into your pocket (though Marzieh doesn't). Bake it the night before, stick it in your pocket, stride down the pavement, let your *hijab* hang lopsided so you'll feel some wind in your hair, and take a bite out of the madeleine with the rap playing for you. Carry out a tiny act of feminism in the name of Marzieh Amiri.

INGREDIENTS

3 eggs
1 tsp baking powder
115g melted butter
115g flour
115g sugar
½ tsp vanilla
55g ground pistachios, ground walnuts, or powdered coconut

DIRECTIONS

Stir together the flour, sugar and baking powder. Beat the eggs and mix with the dry ingredients. Gradually add the melted butter, vanilla and your ground ingredients, whether using walnuts, pistachios or coconut. Cover the mixture and put in the refrigerator for 1 hour. Grease the moulds; fill each two-thirds of the way up, and put them in a 180°C oven for 10–15 minutes, or until the tops have risen and turned a pretty golden colour.

If you haven't baked madeleines before, I'd suggest using walnut powder. It gives the tops a crispness that's just right, not so hard you break your teeth, and it also helps the cakes to come out of their moulds without crumbling, so you can tell the world you're a professional. If you're in prison, you can grind the walnuts yourself using the back of a sieve.

◆ ◆ ◆

TWELVE
Patisserie Pang

'On this day, 5 May, 2021, Patisserie Pang* opened its doors ...'

Mahboubeh Rezaei[†] and the young woman turn towards Roya and aim. *Pang! Pang!* They stare at Arezoo. *Pang! Pang!* They gaze in the wake of a six-year-old sum of 80 million *tomans* ($1,400) and *pang! pang!* at the 700-kilometre point of a dead-end road, *pang! pang!* at the high, deserted staircase, at the 5 a.m. reveille. *Pang! Pang!* at the number of days gone by without a furlough. *Pang!* at the 3,589 people who killed themselves in 2020.

---

* In the local dialect of Bushehr, *pang* is the word for a cluster of fruiting dates.
† Mahboubeh Rezaei, a political and civil rights activist, was first arrested in May 2017 and jailed for two-and-a-half years. She has since been rearrested and now faces another six years in prison for 'removing her hijab', 'propaganda against the regime', 'assembly and collusion against national security', and 'insulting Islamic sanctities'.

Pang! at the harassment, the deserted streets, at the motorbike riders, *pang!* at the number thirteen and Maryam Akbari Monfared, at the graveyard, at Covid-19, at the deaths of millions of people, and *pang! pang!* at the molestation in the corner of the quarantine ward, *pang! pang!* at war and death and Palestine. *Pang!* at colonialism, at bullets. *Pang! Pang!* at the mother tongue* and Article 15 of the Constitution and handcuffs. *Pang! Pang!* at the fish, at fishing, and, finally, the fishermen. *Pang! Pang! Pang!* at World Wetlands Day and the trepidation of waiting to receive a message about the wetlands, and *pang! pang!* at philosophising without having read a single line of philosophy from any philosopher, ever, and *pang! pang!* at their heavy hearts, at nostalgia and separation, at the 38 percent death rate from heart disease and the certainty that, without you, we'll be part of that 38 percent, too. *Pang! Pang!* at 13,000 Syrian children, at bombs and bullets. *Pang!* at the women of Afghanistan and the women of the Taliban. *Pang!* at the gallows and appealing to the cat's

---

* Article 15 of the Islamic Republic's Constitution rules that, despite the multiplicity of languages in use in Iran, Persian is the only one that can be used in official documents, correspondence and textbooks.

hair and the camel's fur for a pardon. *Pang! Pang!* at the forced *hijab* and *chador* in the prison yard, *pang!* at the deserted hallway and the sound of the man breathing in your ear and the panic. *Pang!* at the end of the line, *pang!* at the examinations of your vagina and the public virginity checks … *pang! pang!*

The young woman and Mahboubeh can see that the world is drowned in massacres. By the time the tenth anniversary of Patisserie Pang rolls around, there's every chance Maryam will still be here. The people of Palestine will still be defending their lands with stones. The Yemeni children will have been dead before they could even pronounce *pang*, let alone eat it. Mahboubeh and her young friend have no expectation of praise for founding Patisserie Pang. On the contrary, they're ready for the worst – a treatise perhaps, on the inextricable relationship between *pang* and depravity. They couldn't care less. The point was always this: now that there is no hope of securing a pardon for Kobra Behyari, the least they can do for her is bake her favourite pastry. They'll laugh, eat Swiss rolls, and dance a little here, mere steps away from the gallows.

Recipe 16

Swiss roll
for Mahboubeh Rezaei

◆ ◆ ◆

INGREDIENTS

120g flour
100g sugar
½ tsp vanilla
½ tsp baking powder
4 eggs

25g cooking oil
1 tbsp honey or syrup
a good quantity of
  crème pâtissière
  (see p. 93)

DIRECTIONS

Separate out the egg yolks and whites. Mix the egg yolks with the sugar and vanilla and stir until the result is creamy-coloured and stretchy, then add the honey or syrup. Add the cooking oil and bit by bit sift in the flour and baking powder, stirring vigorously. In a separate bowl, whisk the egg whites until frothy. Gently fold them in.

Pour the mixture into a lined 30cm × 40cm tin and put in a 180°C oven for 10 minutes (only a short stint, so the cake doesn't dry out). Take it out and quickly lay a clean cloth over the top, again to prevent drying. Once it's cooled down, turn the tin upside down and let it drop onto the cloth. Roll it up and leave it to stand for 30 minutes.

In the meantime, make the *crème pât'*. Then unroll the cloth, remove it, cover the mixture with the *crème pât'*, and roll the whole thing up again. Decorate with heavy whipping cream, fruit, or whatever else you like.

◆ ◆ ◆

PATISSERIE PANG

IN THE END, of course, they'll shut down the patisserie. They'll seal away all our dreams and all our *pangs*. Before that happens, though, the night we open the patisserie, Hoda Moradifar reads a poem aloud. Hopefully, it'll be enough to show you what it meant to us:

> We, the noblest of creatures, are strange;
> we are hopeful, likewise lonely, likewise together.
> Humans live only on hope;
> were there no hope, we would end it all.
> We, the women, are lonely and dejected in the corner
>   of this cage;
> we, all of us, are united, attached to one other.
> Together we launch Patisserie Pang
> to sweeten our palates and cheer our souls,
> so the mountain of hope remains unshaken,
> so we'll have a good time here together.
> Hand in hand, we put our trust in God;
> we tear through the billows of misfortune, together,
> hope that the sweetness and delight of this night
> sweeten your palate, and your life.

APPENDIX

A Tribute to Houman Jokar

Houman Jokar, born in 1969 in Tehran, is Sepideh Kashani's husband and the director of two non-governmental organisations: the Conservation of Asiatic Cheetahs Project and the Persian Wildlife Heritage Foundation. He was one of nine conservationists arrested in January 2018 by the Islamic Revolutionary Guard Corps (IRGC). After approximately two years in solitary confinement and more than one thousand hours of interrogation and torture, the Revolutionary Court convicted him of 'espionage' on the basis of no evidence whatsoever, and sentenced him to eight years in prison.

At the time of writing, Houman and his wife are still in prison. Both miss each other from behind bars, instead of missing each other from outside and inside.

The environmental journalist Kaveh Faizolahi wrote the following for *Paazan*, a mammalogy quarterly, about a speech by Houman Jokar:

More than anything else, Houman's nervousness and confusion onstage put one in mind of a *danse macabre* ... With the candour of a man who has rebelled against himself, he compared the cheetah to a beloved child for whose life-threatening illness no physician has been able to find a cause. He put himself in the place of the child's father, and laughed a pain-wracked laugh in the face of this injustice. As the sole actor in the final scene of a tragedy, he confessed that, in reality, the subsequent prescription by international experts has not only not improved the situation of the cheetahs, but made it worse.

He gave full vent to his anger then, saying he was sick and tired of hearing economic and ecological arguments for and against the protection of cheetahs. These are only justifications, he said. Then, like a child whose beloved soap bubble has burst in his hand, the magical rainbow inside taken away with it, he insisted – again like a child – that he wants his cheetahs, and he does not care whether or not humans have any use for them. He said he wants his cheetahs to exist because he loves them. As simple as that!

Houman is a member of the Persian Wildlife Heritage Foundation, and has sought for years to protect the environment in his country. If no wind blew in the desert, if no rain fell on the mountains, and if you lost your way in the forest, you would still see Jokar's footprints anywhere that life exists. You could hear his love songs for Nature in Iran.

Once, in response to questions by reporters about the situation of cheetahs in Iran, he said: 'We and the cheetah live on hope.' This single sentence is the essence of his life. Houman Jokar treats Nature as he does oppressed nations, and has always acted to protect it.

For Houman, the oppressed and forgotten natural environs of Iran and oppressed nations are of a kind. They are forgotten but rebellious, suppressed but roaring. Houman understands oppression well, and this distinguishes him from many others of his generation. His youthful spirit and serenity are well known. He never talks about the abuses he has suffered, but takes the suffering of other people and Nature very seriously indeed. He understands the various injustices well.

The indictment against him by the IRGC mentions the presence of Houman and his wife at the 2009 gatherings [following the disputed presidential elections] and evidences this with an email he sent to a friend of his in Afghanistan, in which Houman wrote: 'As you know, we are experiencing a new type of freedom. For many of us, the difference between leader and government, or between colours [of political orientation] is unimportant. What is important is how quickly people changed. Those who until yesterday were concerned only with their own interests came down to the streets for freedom, even if that meant death. This is incredible. For me, this is a huge change, even if the movement can't go any further. Of course, Sepideh and I participated in the protests and, fortunately, we weren't hurt too badly, except for some tear gas and a few baton blows – sweetly painful, as expected. Unfortunately, however, a close friend of ours is now in prison. To understand the atmosphere at the protests, I am attaching a few pictures we took on our phones.'

He ends his email by referring to the clashes that were then also taking place over elections in Afghanistan: 'If I die during post-election unrest in Tehran, I will become a national hero. But what happens if you die during the same events in Afghanistan?'

This short email illustrates Houman's relationship with politics. He is not political in the conventional sense of the word, but in fact his whole being is political. All his friends agree that he is extremely unassuming and humble; but his humility is not performative. It is rooted in reality. He is so humble that, when he speaks of the possibility of dying in the streets, he immediately distances himself from the performative aspect of it.

ABOUT THE AUTHOR

Sepideh Gholian is an Iranian journalist and activist, currently in Evin Prison. She was arrested on 18 November 2018 during a strike by the workers of the Haft Tappeh Sugarcane Complex, and was severely tortured in detention. In 2023, a video of her removing her hijab and calling for the downfall of Khamenei went viral. In April 2024, she announced she was on hunger strike.